MAP SYMBOLS

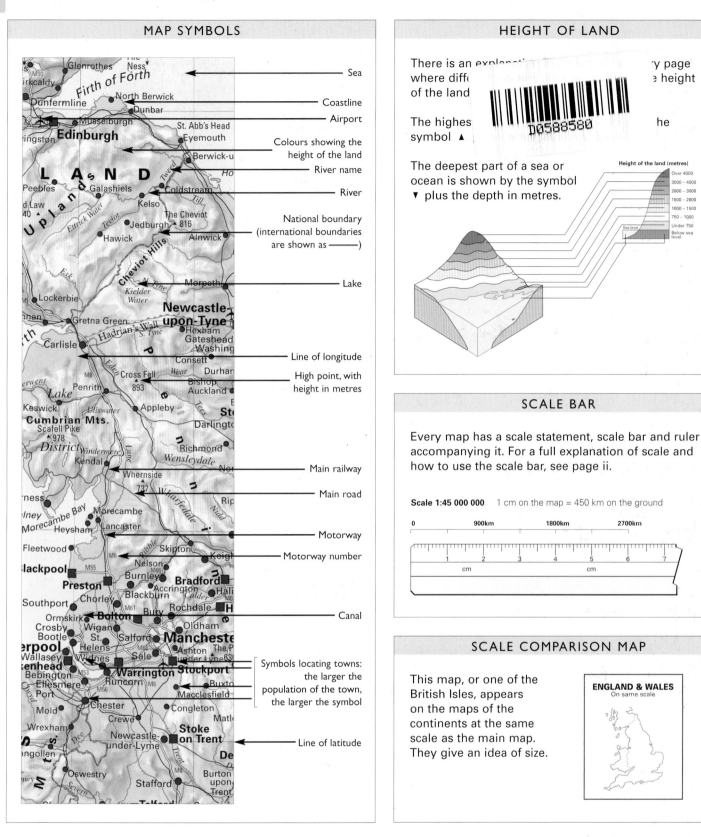

- Sea
- Coastline
- Airport
- Colours showing the height of the land
- River name
- River
- National boundary (international boundaries are shown as ———)
- Lake
- Line of longitude
- High point, with height in metres
- Main railway
- Main road
- Motorway
- Motorway number
- Canal
- Symbols locating towns: the larger the population of the town, the larger the symbol
- Line of latitude

HEIGHT OF LAND

There is an explan... ...ry page where diffe... ...e height of the land...

The highes... ...he symbol ▲...

The deepest part of a sea or ocean is shown by the symbol ▼ plus the depth in metres.

Height of the land (metres)

Over 4000
3000 – 4000
2000 – 3000
1500 – 2000
1000 – 1500
750 – 1000
Under 750
Below sea level

Sea level

SCALE BAR

Every map has a scale statement, scale bar and ruler accompanying it. For a full explanation of scale and how to use the scale bar, see page ii.

Scale 1:45 000 000   1 cm on the map = 450 km on the ground

0	900km	1800km	2700km

1	2	3	4	5	6	7

cm   cm

SCALE COMPARISON MAP

This map, or one of the British Isles, appears on the maps of the continents at the same scale as the main map. They give an idea of size.

ENGLAND & WALES
On same scale

LOCATOR MAP

There is a small map such as this on every map page. The dark green area shows how the main map fits into its larger region.

Philip's World Atlases are published in association with The Royal Geographical Society (with The Institute of British Geographers).

The Society was founded in 1830 and given a Royal Charter in 1859 for 'the advancement of geographical science'. Today it is a leading world centre for geographical learning – supporting education, teaching, research and expeditions, and promoting public understanding of the subject.

Further information about the Society and how to join may be found on its website at: **www.rgs.org**

PHOTOGRAPHIC ACKNOWLEDGEMENTS
© **Crown Copyright** p.vii (map extract)
© **Patricia and Angus Macdonald** p.vi, p.vii
© **NASA/GSFC** p.32 (top right), p.32 (bottom)
© **Courtesy of NPA Group, Edenbridge, UK** p.viii, p.ix, p.2 (top left), p.2 (centre), p.18 (bottom left), p.18 (bottom right), p.24, p.27, p.28
© **Science Photo Library** /JBP/NRSC p.32 (top left), p.32 (centre), /CNES, 1989 Distribution Spot Image p.26, /Geospace p.23, /M-SAT Ltd p.2 (top right), p.2 (bottom), /NRSC Ltd p.31, /PLI pp.18–19 (top), p.33, /RESTEC, Japan p.25, /Tom Van Sant/Geosphere Project, Santa Monica p.17, /WORLDSAT Productions/NRSC p.3
© **Tony Stone Images** p.30
Photographs page 63 (top to bottom): **Britstock-IFA; Zefa Pictures; Robert Harding Picture Library; Finnish Tourist Board; Robert Harding Picture Library; Tony Stone Images**

Scale and Direction

TYPES OF SCALE

In this atlas the scale of the map is shown in three ways:

WRITTEN STATEMENT

This tells you how many kilometres on the Earth are represented by one centimetre on the map.

1 cm on the map = 20 km on the ground

RATIO

This tells you that one unit on the map represents two million of the same unit on the ground.

1:2 000 000

SCALE BAR

This shows you the scale as a line or bar with a section of ruler beneath it.

HOW TO MEASURE DISTANCE

The map on the right is a small part of the map of Southern Europe, which is on page 38 in the World section of the atlas.

The scale of the map extract is shown below:

Scale 1:10 000 000   1 cm on the map = 100 km on the ground

To measure the distance from London to Paris you can use any of the three methods described above.

For example:

USING THE WRITTEN STATEMENT

Using the scale above, you can see that 1 cm on the map represents 100 km on the ground.

Measure the distance on the map between London and Paris. You will see that this is about 3.5 cm.

If 1 cm = 100 km

then 3.5 cm = 350 km (3.5 × 100)

USING THE RATIO

Using the scale above, you can see that the ratio is 1:10 000 000.

We know that the distance on the map between the cities is 3.5 cm and we know from the ratio that 1 cm on the map = 10 000 000 cm on the ground. We multiply the map distance by the ratio.

= 3.5 × 10 000 000 cm
= 35 000 000 cm
= 350 000 m
= **350 km**

USING THE SCALE BAR

We know that the distance on the map between the cities is 3.5 cm.

Using the scale bar, measure 3.5 cm along this (or use the yellow section of the ruler as a guide) and read off the distance.

Using these three methods, now work out the distance between London and Birmingham on the map above. Your teacher could tell you if your answer is correct.

The map on the left is an extract from the map of Asia on page 42 in the World section of the atlas. Below, you can see the scale of this map. See if you can calculate the distance between Kolkata (Calcutta) and Bangkok.

Scale 1:48 000 000   1 cm on the map = 480 km on the ground

DIFFERENT SIZES OF SCALE

The table on the right shows the distances from London to Paris and Bangkok to Kolkata. The map distances are both 3.5 cm, but the actual distances are very different. This is because the maps are at different scales.

On the continent maps, in the World section of this atlas, are **scale comparison maps**. These show you the size of the British Isles drawn at the same scale as the main map on that page. This is to give you an idea of the size of that continent.

	Map Distance	Scale	Actual Distance
London – Paris	3.5 cm	1:10 000 000	350 km
Bangkok – Kolkata	3.5 cm	1:45 000 000	1,575 km

Below are three maps which appear in this atlas:

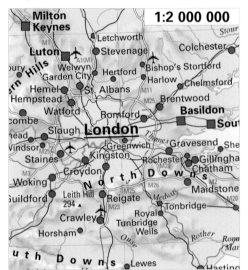

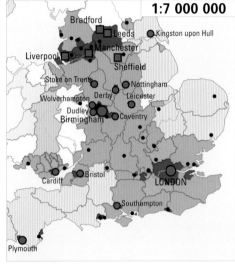

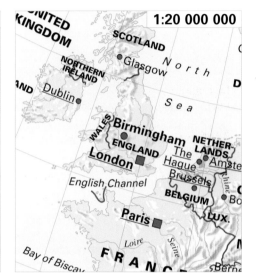

These maps all show London, but the map above shows much more detail than the maps on the right. The map above is a larger-scale map than the maps on the right.

A **large-scale** map shows more detail of a **small** area.

A **small-scale** map shows less detail of a **large** area.

Notice how the ratios are getting larger as the scale of the map gets smaller.

DIRECTION ON THE MAPS

On most of the atlas maps, north is at the top of the page. Longitude lines run from south to north. These usually curve a little because the Earth is a globe and not a flat shape.

POINTS OF THE COMPASS

Below is a drawing of the points of a compass. North, east, south and west are called **cardinal points**. Direction is sometimes given in degrees. This is measured clockwise from north. To help you remember the order of the compass points try to learn this sentence:

Naughty **E**lephants **S**quirt **W**ater

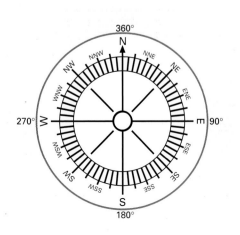

USING A COMPASS

Compasses have a needle with a magnetic tip. The tip is attracted towards the Magnetic North Pole which is close to the North Pole. The compass tells you where north is. You can see the Magnetic North Pole on the diagram below.

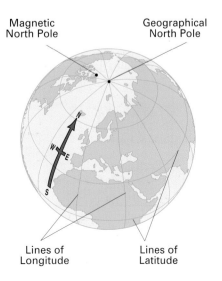

ACTIVITIES

Look at the map below.
If Keswick is south of Edinburgh then:
• Armagh is _____ of Oxford;
• Fort William is _____ of Edinburgh;
• Ilfracombe is _____ of Oxford.
Look at the map on pages 4–5 of the British Isles section:
• Which is the most southerly town shown in England?
• Which is the most westerly town shown in Wales?

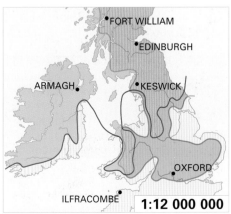

Latitude and Longitude

LATITUDE

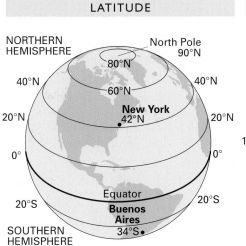

Lines of latitude cross the atlas maps from east to west. The Equator is at 0°. All other lines of latitude are either north of the Equator, or south of the Equator. Line 40°N is almost halfway towards the North Pole. The North Pole is at 90°N. At the Equator, a degree of longitude measures about 110 km.

LONGITUDE

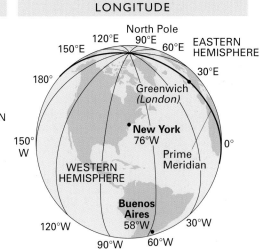

Lines of longitude run from north to south. These lines meet at the North Pole and the South Pole. Longitude 0° passes through Greenwich. This line is also called the Prime Meridian. Lines of longitude are either east of 0° or west of 0°. There are 180 degrees of longitude both east and west of 0°.

USING LATITUDE AND LONGITUDE

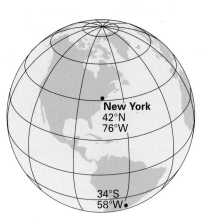

Latitude and longitude lines make a grid. You can find a place if you know its latitude and longitude number. The latitude number is either north or south of the Equator. The longitude number is either east or west of the Greenwich Meridian.

SPECIAL LATITUDE LINES

Some special latitude lines are shown on maps. The diagrams on page 72 of the World section show that the Sun is only overhead vertically in the tropical regions. These regions are between 23°30′ north and 23°30′ south of the Equator. On the maps in this atlas these are shown as blue dotted lines. The **Tropic of Cancer** is at 23°30′N and the **Tropic of Capricorn** is at 23°30′S.

In the North and South Polar regions there are places where the Sun does not rise or set above the horizon at certain times of the year. These places are also shown by a blue dotted line on the maps. The **Arctic Circle** is at 66°30′N and the **Antarctic Circle** is at 66°30′S.

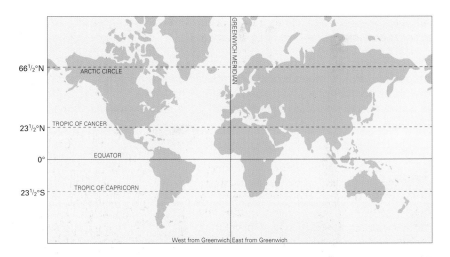

LATITUDE AND LONGITUDE IN THIS ATLAS

In this atlas lines of latitude and longitude are coloured blue.

On large-scale maps, such as those in the British Isles section (pages 4–7), there is a line for every degree. On smaller-scale maps only every other, every fifth or even tenth line is shown.

The map on the right shows the British Isles. The latitude and longitude lines are numbered at the edges of the map. The bottom of the map shows whether a place is east or west of Greenwich. The side of the map tells you how far north from the Equator the line is.

Around the edges of the map are small yellow pointers with letters and numbers in their boxes. Columns made by longitude lines have letters in their boxes; rows made by latitude lines have numbers.

In the index at the end of the atlas, places have number-letter references as well as latitude and longitude numbers to help you locate the place names on the maps.

On the map opposite, London is in rectangle **8M** (this is where row 8 crosses with column M). Edinburgh is in **4J** and Dublin is in **6F**.

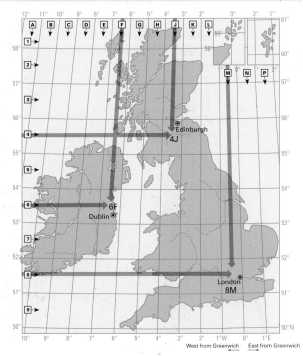

HOW TO FIND A PLACE

The map on the right is an extract from the map of Scotland on page 6 of the British Isles section. If you want to find Stornoway in the atlas, you must look in the index. Places are listed alphabetically. You will find the following entry:

Stornoway .... **6** **1B** 58°N 6°W

The number in **bold** type is the page number where the map appears. The figure and letter which follow the page number give the grid rectangle on the map in which the feature appears. Here we can see that Stornoway is on page 6 in the rectangle where row 1 crosses column B.

The latitude and longitude number corresponds with the numbered lines on the map. The first set of figures represent the latitude and the second set represent the longitude. The unit of measurement for latitude and longitude is the degree (°) which is divided into minutes ('). Here, only full degrees are given.

Latitude and longitude can be used to locate places more accurately on smaller-scale maps such as those in the World section.

All rivers are indexed to their mouth or confluence and in the index they are followed by the symbol ➔ .

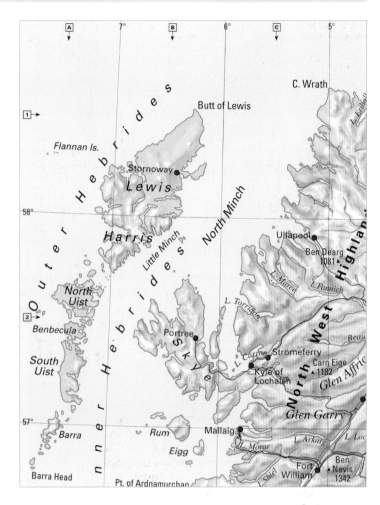

MAKING MAPS

One of the greatest problems in making maps is how to draw the curved surface of the globe on a flat piece of paper. This map (right) shows one way of putting the globe on to paper, but because it splits up the land and sea it is not very useful.

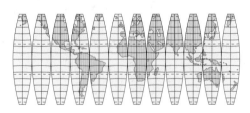

This map (right) is better. It is a good map because it shows the correct size of places. It is an **equal-area map**. For example, Australia is the correct size in relation to North America, and Europe is the correct size in relation to Africa. Comparing areas is a useful way of checking the accuracy of maps. Comparing Greenland (2.2 million km²) with Australia (7.7 million km²) is a good 'area test'.

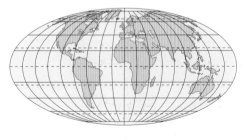

In this atlas most maps are reasonable for area and scale. Latitude lines are curves and longitude lines are straight lines or curves.

The map below is called **Mercator**. It has been used since the 16th century. The area scale is not equal area. Many sea and air maps are drawn on this type of map.

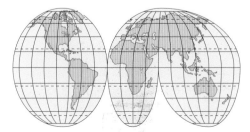

A better shape at the edges of the map can be made by splitting the map (left).

The scale of distances is difficult to put on a map. On the left-hand map, the Equator and Greenwich Meridian are true to scale. On the Mercator map (right), scale is correct along the Equator but is less correct towards the Poles.

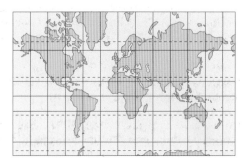

Edinburgh Street Map
Key to Map Symbols

Symbol	Description		Symbol	Description
	Motorway			Shopping Streets
	Primary Route Dual/Single			Railway
	Main Road Dual/Single			Tramway with Station
	Secondary Road Dual/Single			Railway/ Bus Station
	Minor Through Road/One Way Street			Shopping Precinct/ Retail Park
	Pedestrian Roads			Park
	Abbey/Cathedral			Shopmobility
	Art Gallery			Theatre
	Building of Public Interest			Tourist Information Centre
	Castle			Other Place of Interest
	Church of interest			Hospital
	Cinema			Parking
	House			Police
	Museum			Post Office
	Railway Station			

COPYRIGHT PHIL

Scale 1:10 000   1 cm on the map and aerial photograph = 100 metres on the ground

Edinburgh

| 0 | | | | 500 metres | | | | | 1 km |

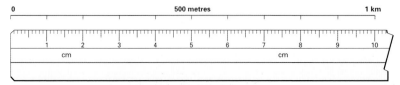

O.S. Explorer Map of St. Ives

Key to Map Symbols

Roads and Paths

A 31(T)	Trunk or main road
B 3074	Secondary road
	Road more than 4 metres wide
	Road less than 4 metres wide
	Other road, drive or track
	Path
	Public right of way

Railways

	Single track
	Cutting, embankment

Symbols

▪ ▪ +	Place of worship
▢ ▢	Building, important building
⚲ ⚲	Lighthouse, beacon
△	Triangulation pillar
○ W, Spr	Well, spring
~~	Cliff
▢ ▢	Water, sand and shingle

Vegetation

	Coniferous forest
	Non-coniferous forest
	Coppice
	Orchard
	Scrub
	Bracken, rough grassland

Heights

˙116	Spot heights in metres
	Contours are in 5 metre intervals

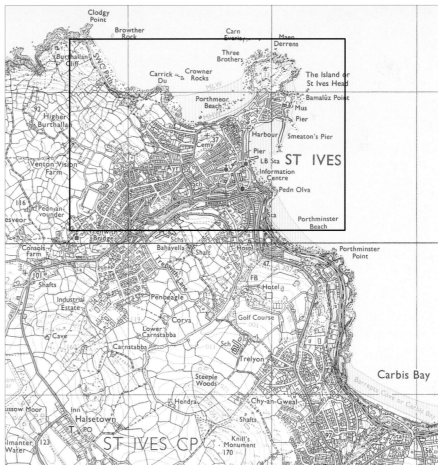

Reproduced from the 1992 Ordnance Survey 1:25,000 scale map with the permission of the Controller of Her Majesty's Stationery Office © Crown Copyright

Scale of photograph 1:10 000

500 metres

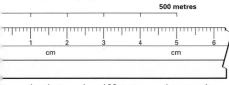

cm on the photograph = 100 metres on the ground

Scale of map 1:25 000

0   500 metres   1 km   1.5 km

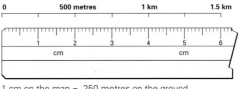

1 cm on the map = 250 metres on the ground

St. Ives

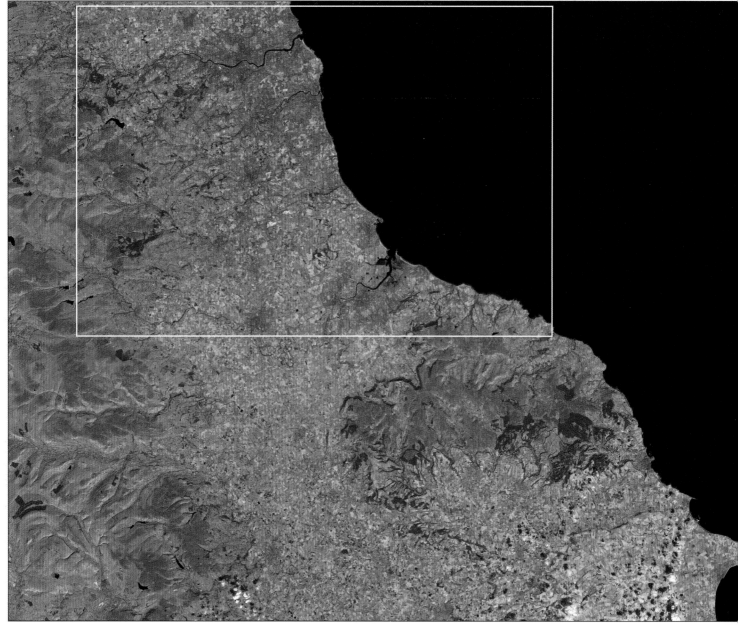

Landsat images

The images on these pages were produced by the Landsat 5 satellite, launched by NASA in 1984. It travels around the Earth at a height of over 700 km. It is able to scan every part of the Earth's surface once every 16 days. The data is transmitted back to Earth where it is printed in false colours to make certain features stand out.

On these pages grass and crops appear red, soils and exposed rock light blue, woodland dark red, moorland brown, water black and built-up areas dark-grey. The image on page viii shows North-east England and the image on page ix shows North Wales. Both images were recorded in late September. Comparing the maps with the images helps to identify specific features on the images.

Scale 1:760 000   1 cm on the map and satellite image = 7.6 km on the ground

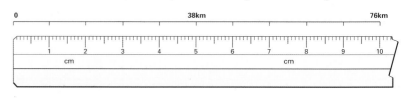

Key to Map Symbols

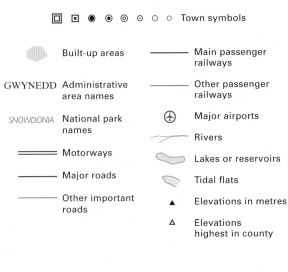

▣ ▢ ◉ ◉ ◎ ⊙ ○ ○ Town symbols

Built-up areas

GWYNEDD Administrative area names

SNOWDONIA National park names

═══ Motorways

─── Major roads

─── Other important roads

─── Main passenger railways

─── Other passenger railways

✈ Major airports

Rivers

Lakes or reservoirs

Tidal flats

▲ Elevations in metres

△ Elevations highest in county

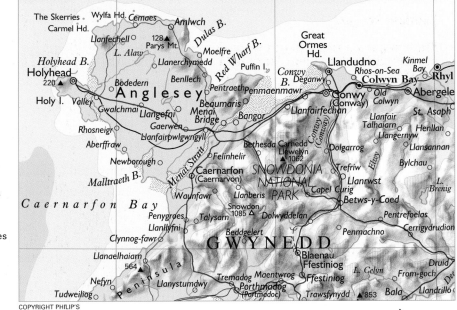

The Skerries Wylfa Hd. Cemaes Amlwch
Carmel Hd. Dulas B.
Llanfechell 128▲ Moelfre Red Wharf B. Great Ormes Hd.
Parys Mt. Llandudno Kinmel Bay
Holyhead B. L. Alaw Llanerchymedd Puffin I. Conwy Rhos-on-Sea Bay
Holyhead Benllech B. Deganwy Colwyn Bay Rhyl
220▲ Bodedern Pentraeth Penmaenmawr Conwy Old Abergele
Holy I. Valley **Anglesey** (Conway) Colwyn
Gwalchmai Beaumaris Llanfairfechan Llanfair St. Asaph
Rhosneigr Llangefni Menai Bangor Talhaiarn Henllan
Gaerwen Bridge Llangernyw
Aberffraw Llanfairpwllgwyngyll Bethesda Carnedd Dolgarrog Llansannan
Newborough Felinheli Llewelyn Trefriw Bylchau
1062▲ **SNOWDONIA**
Malltraeth B. Caernarfon **NATIONAL** Llanrwst L.
(Caernarvon) **PARK** Capel Curig Brenig
Caernarfon Bay Waunfawr Llanberis Betws-y-Coed
Penygroes Talysarn Snowdon Dolwyddelan Pentrefoelas
Llanllyfni 1085△ Penmachno Cerrigydrudion
Clynnog-fawr Beddgelert **GWYNEDD**
Llanaelhaiarn Blaenau Druid
564▲ Ffestiniog L. Celyn From-goch
Nefyn *Peninsula* Tremadog Maentwrog Ffestiniog Bala
Llanystumdwy Porthmadog Trawsfynydd 853▲ Llandrillo
Tudweiliog (Portmadoc)

COPYRIGHT PHILIP'S

Scale 1:760 000 1 cm on the map and satellite image = 7.6 km on the ground

0 ─────── 38km ─────── 76km

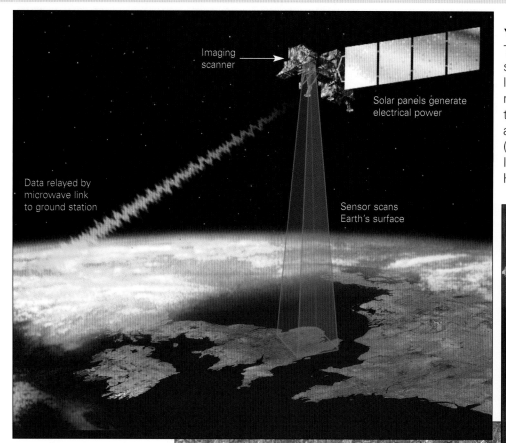

Imaging
scanner

Solar panels generate
electrical power

Data relayed by
microwave link
to ground station

Sensor scans
Earth's surface

▼ Western Scotland

The brown region indicates the sparsely-populated Highland region lying north of Glasgow. Around the rugged coastline (which includes the Firth of Clyde, Firth of Lorn and Loch Fyne), the islands of Mull (centre left), Jura (lower left) and Islay (bottom left) form part of the Hebrides archipelago.

▲ Earth Observation Satellites

Powered by outstretched solar panels, Earth Observation Satellites, such as the one shown above, record images of the Earth's surface and relay the images digitally to ground-receiving stations.

▶ The Thames Basin and London

This Landsat satellite image clearly shows the extent of the Greater London conurbation. The runways of Heathrow Airport are clearly visible at centre left.

◀ Southern England

This true-colour satellite image shows the Isle of Wight (bottom left) separated from the mainland by the Solent. Parts of the counties of Hampshire and West Sussex appear on the image, with the major towns of Southampton (far left), Portsmouth (lower left) and Brighton (lower right) all clearly visible.

The British Isles seen from Space
A mosaic of data gathered by Landsat satellites, the colours on this image have been processed to match the natural tone of the landscape. The large amount of agricultural land in the UK is reflected by the extensive brownish green on the image. In Scotland, snow-covered mountains are seen, with dark-green coniferous forests below the snow line. Most of Ireland has a mid-green colour which indicates the presence of rich pasture.

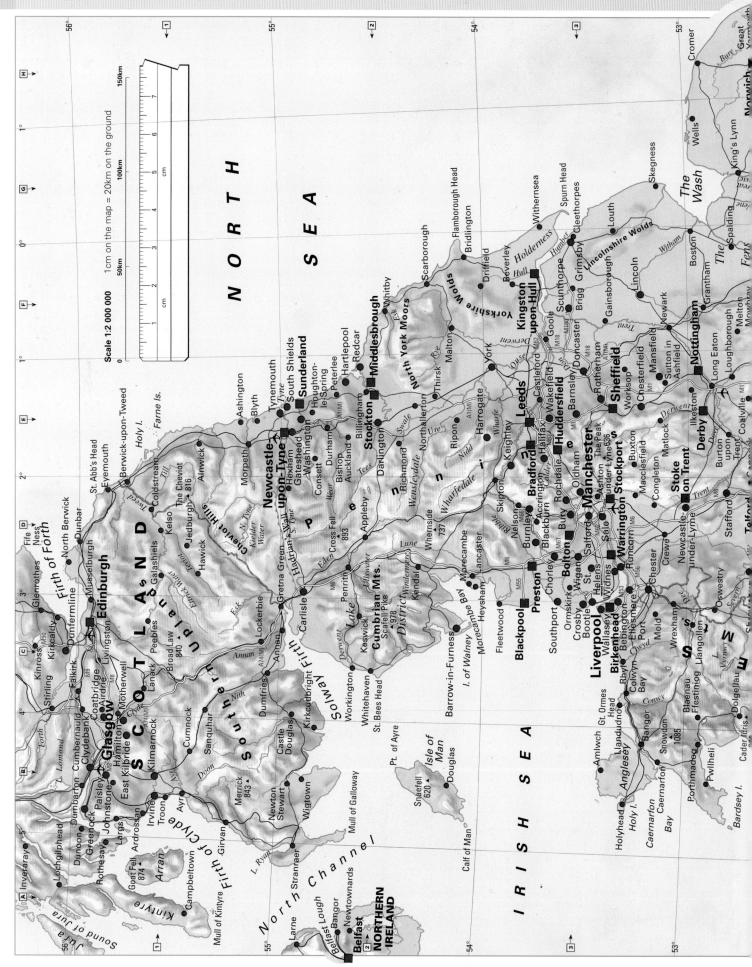

Scale 1:2 000 000

1cm on the map = 20km on the ground

0 cm 1 2 3 4 5 6 7

0 50km 100km 150km

N O R T H   S E A

I R I S H   S E A

North Channel

Sound of Jura

Firth of Forth

Firth of Clyde

S C O T L A N D

NORTHERN IRELAND

Belfast

Glasgow

Edinburgh

Newcastle upon-Tyne

Middlesbrough

Sunderland

Leeds

Bradford

Manchester

Liverpool

Sheffield

Kingston upon-Hull

Nottingham

Derby

Stoke-on-Trent

Blackpool

Preston

Warrington

Birkenhead

Stockport

Huddersfield

Cumbrian Mts.

Lake District

Pennines

The Wash

Isle of Man

Anglesey

Snowdon 1085

Lincolnshire Wolds

Yorkshire Wolds

North York Moors

Cheviot Hills

Southern Uplands

Norwich

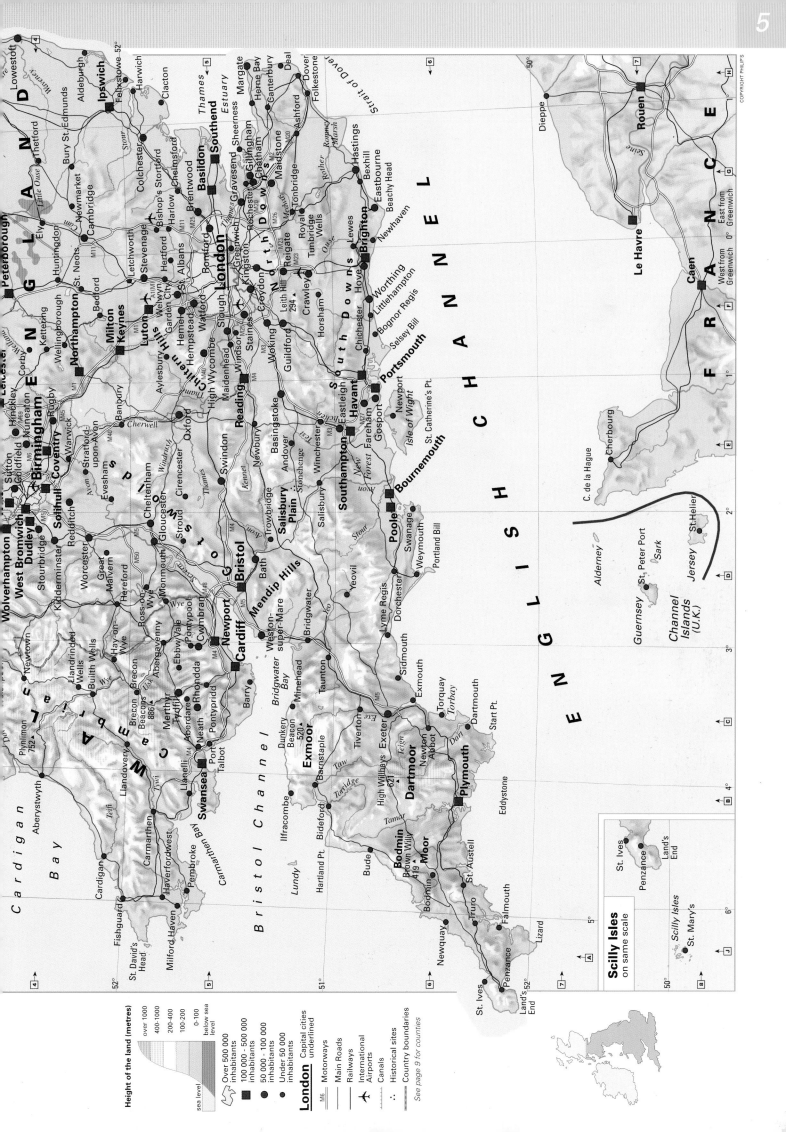

Height of the land (metres)

	over 1000
	400–1000
	200–400
	100–200
	0–100
sea level	below sea level

- ☐ Over 500 000 inhabitants
- ■ 100 000 - 500 000 inhabitants
- ● 50 000 - 100 000 inhabitants
- • Under 50 000 inhabitants

London Capital cities underlined

M6	Motorways
	Main Roads
	Railways
✈	International Airports
	Canals
∴	Historical sites
	Country boundaries

See page 9 for counties

Scilly Isles on same scale

St. Ives
Penzance
Land's End

Scilly Isles
St. Mary's

COPYRIGHT PHILIP'S

ENGLAND
WALES
FRANCE

ENGLISH CHANNEL

Bristol Channel

Cardigan Bay

Strait of Dover
Thames Estuary

North Downs
South Downs
Chiltern Hills
Salisbury Plain
Mendip Hills
Cotswold Hills
Exmoor
Dartmoor
Bodmin Moor
New Forest
Brecon Beacons
Romney Marsh

Lowestoft
Waveney
Ipswich
Felixstowe
Harwich
Clacton
Deal
Margate
Herne Bay
Canterbury
Folkestone
Dover
Aldeburgh
Thetford
Bury St. Edmunds
Newmarket
Colchester
Bishop's Stortford
Harlow
Chelmsford
Brentwood
Basildon
Southend
Sheerness
Gillingham
Gravesend
Chatham
Rochester
Maidstone
Ashford
Hastings
Bexhill
Eastbourne
Beachy Head
Tonbridge
Royal Tunbridge Wells
Lewes
Newhaven
Brighton
Hove
Worthing
Littlehampton
Bognor Regis
Selsey Bill
Chichester
Peterborough
Ely
Little Ouse
Cambridge
St. Neots
Huntingdon
Bedford
Letchworth
Stevenage
Hertford
St. Albans
Welwyn Garden City
Hemel Hempstead
Watford
Hatfield
London
Greenwich
Kingston
Croydon
Reigate
Redhill
Leith Hill 294
Crawley
Horsham
Milton Keynes
Luton
Northampton
Wellingborough
Kettering
Corby
Leicester
Hinckley
Nuneaton
Rugby
Warwick
Coventry
Birmingham
Solihull
Sutton Coldfield
West Bromwich
Dudley
Wolverhampton
Stourbridge
Kidderminster
Redditch
Worcester
Great Malvern
Hereford
Ross-on-Wye
Monmouth
Gloucester
Cheltenham
Stroud
Cirencester
Swindon
Oxford
Banbury
Stratford-upon-Avon
Evesham
Aylesbury
High Wycombe
Maidenhead
Windsor
Slough
Staines
Reading
Newbury
Basingstoke
Andover
Winchester
Southampton
Eastleigh
Fareham
Gosport
Portsmouth
Havant
Newport
Isle of Wight
St. Catherine's Pt.
Bournemouth
Poole
Swanage
Weymouth
Portland Bill
Dorchester
Lyme Regis
Sidmouth
Exmouth
Exeter
Tiverton
Torquay
Torbay
Dartmouth
Start Pt.
Newton Abbot
Plymouth
Eddystone
Bodmin
Brown Willy 419
Bude
Bideford
Barnstaple
Ilfracombe
Hartland Pt.
Lundy
Minehead
Bridgwater
Taunton
Yeovil
Salisbury
Trowbridge
Bath
Bristol
Weston-super-Mare
Bridgwater Bay
Newport
Cardiff
Barry
Cwmbran
Pontypool
Abergavenny
Ebbw Vale
Rhondda
Aberdare
Merthyr Tydfil
Pontypridd
Neath
Port Talbot
Swansea
Llanelli
Carmarthen
Llandovery
Brecon
Builth Wells
Llandrindod Wells
Newtown
Aberystwyth
Cardigan
Fishguard
Haverfordwest
Milford Haven
Pembroke
Carmarthen Bay
Pembroke Bay
St. David's Head
Plynlimon 752
Dunkery Beacon 520
High Willhays 621
Dartmoor 621
Newquay
St. Austell
Truro
Falmouth
Lizard
St. Ives
Penzance
Land's End

Le Havre
Caen
Rouen
Dieppe
Cherbourg
C. de la Hague
Alderney
Guernsey
St. Peter Port
Sark
Jersey
St. Helier
Channel Islands (U.K.)

Wolverhampton
Seine

East from Greenwich
West from Greenwich 0°

Scotland

Shetland Is.
on same scale

Orkney Is.
on same scale

Scale 1:2 000 000   1cm on the map = 20km on the ground

| 0 | 50km | 100km | 150km | 200km |

COPYRIGHT PHILIP'S

Height of the land (metres)

over 1000	
400-1000	
200-400	
100-200	
0-100	
sea level	below sea level

⌂ Over 500 000 inhabitants

■ 100 000 - 500 000 inhabitants

● 50 000 - 100 000 inhabitants

● Under 50 000 inhabitants

Dublin Capital cities underlined

M6 Motorways

Main Roads

Railways

✈ International Airports

Canals

Country boundaries

COPYRIGHT PHILIP'S

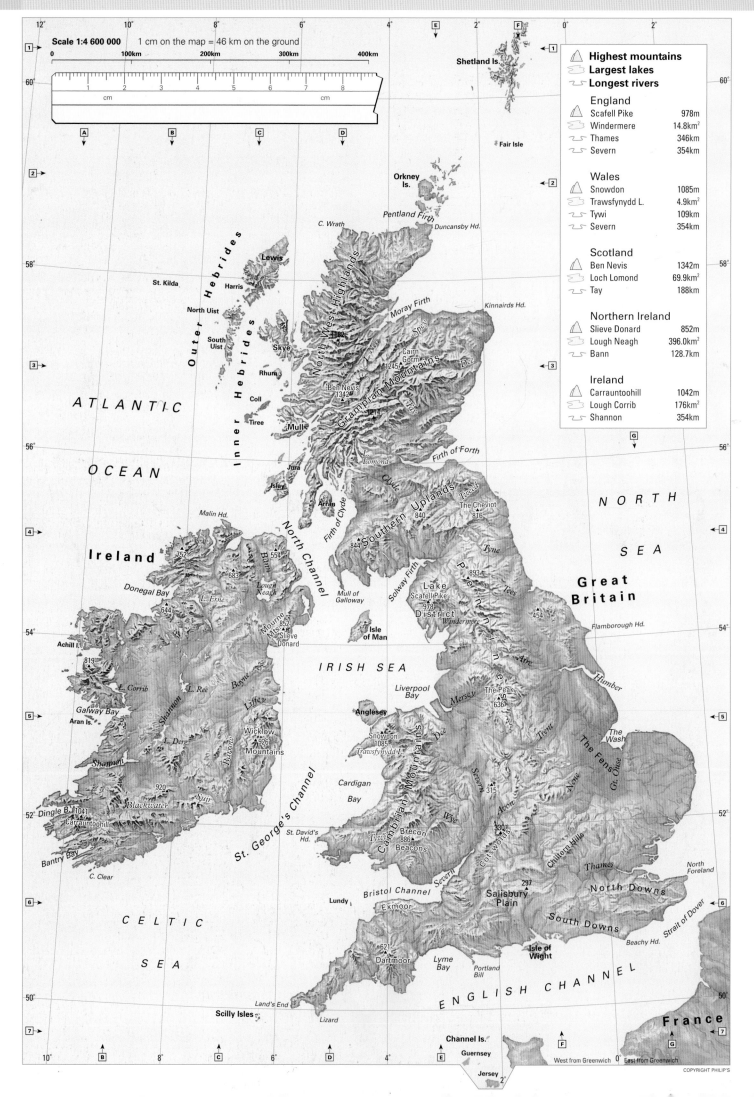

Scale 1:4 600 000   1 cm on the map = 46 km on the ground

0   100km   200km   300km   400km

cm   cm

Shetland Is.

Fair Isle

Highest mountains
Largest lakes
Longest rivers

England
Scafell Pike   978m
Windermere   14.8km²
Thames   346km
Severn   354km

Wales
Snowdon   1085m
Trawsfynydd L.   4.9km²
Tywi   109km
Severn   354km

Scotland
Ben Nevis   1342m
Loch Lomond   69.9km²
Tay   188km

Northern Ireland
Slieve Donard   852m
Lough Neagh   396.0km²
Bann   128.7km

Ireland
Carrauntoohill   1042m
Lough Corrib   176km²
Shannon   354km

Orkney Is.

Pentland Firth

C. Wrath   Duncansby Hd.

Outer Hebrides

Lewis

St. Kilda

Harris

North Uist

Moray Firth   Kinnairds Hd.

South Uist

Inner Hebrides

North West Highlands

1182

Skye

Cairn Gorm 1245

Spey

Dee

Rhum

Ben Nevis 1342

Coll

1214

Tay

Grampian Mountains

ATLANTIC

Tiree

Mull

OCEAN

L. Lomond

Firth of Forth

Jura

Clyde

Islay

Tweed

Arran

Firth of Clyde

Southern Uplands

The Cheviot 816

NORTH

Malin Hd.

840

844

Tyne

SEA

Ireland

752

554

Mull of Galloway

Solway Firth

Tees

Great Britain

683

Barrow

Lough Neagh

Lake District

893

Donegal Bay

L. Erne

644

North Channel

Scafell Pike 978

454

Flamborough Hd.

Mourne Mts. 852

Isle of Man

Windermere

Achill I.

Slieve Donard

IRISH SEA

819

Aire

L. Corrib

L. Ree

Boyne

Liverpool Bay

The Peak 636

Humber

Galway Bay

Shannon

Liffey

Mersey

Pennines

Aran Is.

L. Derg

Barrow

Wicklow

Anglesey

Dee

Trent

The Wash

920

Suir

926

Mountains

Snowdon 1085

Severn

The Fens

Shannon

Blackwater

Trawsfynydd L.

Gt. Ouse

Cardigan Bay

315

Nene

Dingle B. 1041

Cambrian Mountains

Wye

330

Carrauntoohill

Tywi

Avon

Chiltern Hills

St. George's Channel

Brecon 886 Beacons

Cotswolds

Thames

North Foreland

Bantry Bay

St. David's Hd.

Severn

297

North Downs

C. Clear

Bristol Channel

Salisbury Plain

South Downs

CELTIC

Lundy

Exmoor

Beachy Hd.

Strait of Dover

621

SEA

Dartmoor

Lyme Bay

Isle of Wight

Portland Bill

Land's End

ENGLISH CHANNEL

Scilly Isles

Lizard

France

Channel Is.

West from Greenwich   0°   East from Greenwich

Guernsey

Jersey

COPYRIGHT PHILIP'S

COUNTRY FACTS

Country Name	Area (square kilometres)	Inhabitants (thousands 2001)	Capital City or Town
UNITED KINGDOM	**240,883**	**58,837**	**LONDON**
of which England	129,652	49,181	London
Wales	20,628	2,903	Cardiff
Scotland	77,097	5,064	Edinburgh
N. Ireland	13,532	1,689	Belfast
*Isle of Man	572	76	Douglas
* Jersey	116	89	St. Helier
*Guernsey	63	64	St. Peter Port
IRELAND	**68,896**	**3,897**	**DUBLIN**

* Crown Dependencies which are not part of the U.K.

The map shows the 6 counties in Northern Ireland, the 32 unitary authorities in Scotland, the 22 unitary authorities in Wales and the 87 unitary authorities in England as of 1st April 1998. Authorities which are too small to name on the map are numbered and listed separately.

SCOTLAND
1. ABERDEEN CITY
2. DUNDEE CITY
3. WEST DUNBARTONSHIRE
4. EAST DUNBARTONSHIRE
5. CITY OF GLASGOW
6. INVERCLYDE
7. RENFREWSHIRE
8. EAST RENFREWSHIRE
9. NORTH LANARKSHIRE
10. FALKIRK
11. CLACKMANNANSHIRE
12. WEST LOTHIAN
13. CITY OF EDINBURGH
14. MIDLOTHIAN

● Capital cities

The Channel Islands and the Isle of Man are dependencies of the Crown and have their own parliaments. They are not part of the United Kingdom.

WALES
15. SWANSEA
16. NEATH PORT TALBOT
17. BRIDGEND
18. RHONDDA CYNON TAFF
19. MERTHYR TYDFIL
20. CAERPHILLY
21. BLAENAU GWENT
22. TORFAEN
23. CARDIFF
24. NEWPORT

ENGLAND
25. HARTLEPOOL
26. DARLINGTON
27. STOCKTON-ON-TEES
28. MIDDLESBROUGH
29. REDCAR AND CLEVELAND
30. BLACKPOOL
31. BLACKBURN WITH DARWEN
32. HALTON
33. WARRINGTON
34. KINGSTON UPON HULL
35. NORTH EAST LINCOLNSHIRE
36. STOKE-ON-TRENT
37. TELFORD AND WREKIN
38. DERBY CITY
39. CITY OF NOTTINGHAM
40. LEICESTER CITY
41. RUTLAND
42. PETERBOROUGH
43. MILTON KEYNES
44. LUTON
45. NORTH SOMERSET
46. CITY OF BRISTOL
47. BATH AND N. E. SOMERSET
48. SWINDON
49. READING
50. WOKINGHAM
51. WINDSOR AND MAIDENHEAD
52. SLOUGH
53. BRACKNELL FOREST
54. THURROCK
55. SOUTHEND-ON-SEA
56. MEDWAY
57. PLYMOUTH
58. TORBAY
59. POOLE
60. BOURNEMOUTH
61. SOUTHAMPTON
62. PORTSMOUTH
63. BRIGHTON AND HOVE

COPYRIGHT PHILIP'S

Weather is measured in terms of rainfall, temperature, cloudiness, sunshine and wind over a short period of time, usually less than a day. Climate is the average of the weather over a longer period, usually 30 years.

CLIMATE MAP

— 4°C in January
— 15°C in July
Cool summer, cold winter
Cool summer, mild winter
Warm summer, cool winter
Warm summer, mild winter

RENFREW
°C
30 20 10 0 -10 -20 -30 -40
Temperature
Rainfall 1109mm
350 300 250 200 150 100 50 mm
J F M A M J J A S O N D

BELFAST
°C
30 20 10 0 -10 -20 -30 -40
Temperature
Rainfall 845mm
350 300 250 200 150 100 50 mm
J F M A M J J A S O N D

CROMER
°C
30 20 10 0 -10 -20 -30 -40
Temperature
Rainfall 618mm
350 300 250 200 150 100 50 mm
J F M A M J J A S O N D

AMBLESIDE
°C
30 20 10 0 -10 -20 -30 -40
Temperature
Rainfall 1851mm
350 300 250 200 150 100 50 mm
J F M A M J J A S O N D

VALENCIA
°C
30 20 10 0 -10 -20 -30 -40
Temperature
Rainfall 1400mm
350 300 250 200 150 100 50 mm
J F M A M J J A S O N D

PLYMOUTH
°C
30 20 10 0 -10 -20 -30 -40
Temperature
Rainfall 950mm
350 300 250 200 150 100 50 mm
J F M A M J J A S O N D

CLIMATE GRAPHS

Colour of climate region on map
Name of town
Average monthly daily maximum temperature
Average monthly temperature
Average monthly daily minimum temperature
Average annual rainfall
Average monthly rainfall
Months of the year

OXFORD
°C
30 20 10 0 -10 -20 -30 -40
Temperature
Rainfall 660mm
350 300 250 200 150 100 50 mm
J F M A M J J A S O N D

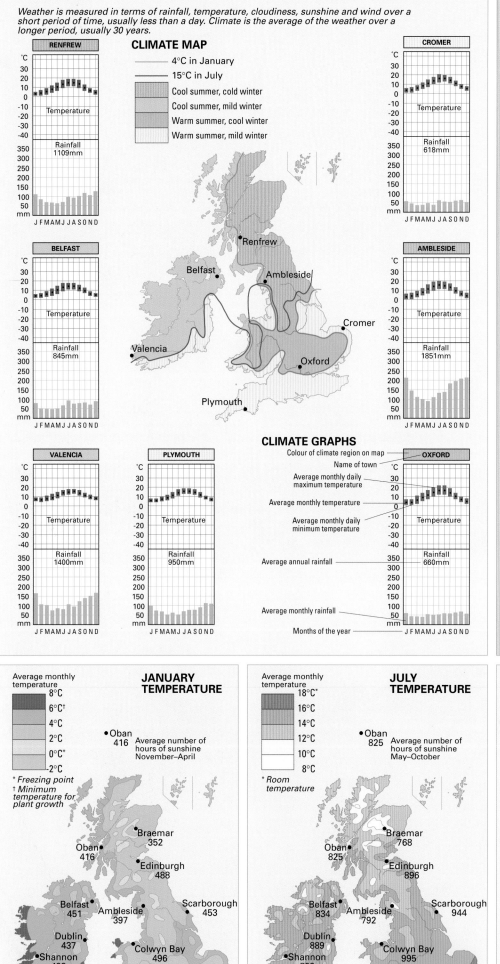

Map labels: Renfrew, Belfast, Ambleside, Cromer, Valencia, Oxford, Plymouth

WEATHER MAP

The map below shows the types of symbols used in weather forecasts on television and in newspapers.

2 Temperature in degrees Celsius above freezing point (0° Celsius)
1 Temperature in degrees Celsius below freezing point (0° Celsius)
7 Sunshine with temperature in degrees Celsius
Thin cloud, fine weather
Thick cloud, dull weather
Cloudy with sunny intervals
Rain
Rain showers with sunny intervals
Snow
Sleet
Thunderstorms with lightning
5→ Wind direction and speed in miles per hour
FOG Fog

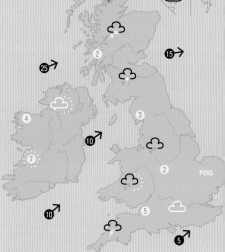

JANUARY TEMPERATURE

Average monthly temperature
8°C
6°C †
4°C
2°C
0°C *
-2°C

* Freezing point
† Minimum temperature for plant growth

●Oban 416 Average number of hours of sunshine November–April

Braemar 352
Oban 416
Edinburgh 488
Belfast 451
Ambleside 397
Dublin 437
Shannon 493
Scarborough 453
Colwyn Bay 496
Birmingham 424
Kew 476
Newquay 575
Bournemouth 593

JULY TEMPERATURE

Average monthly temperature
18°C *
16°C
14°C
12°C
10°C
8°C

* Room temperature

●Oban 825 Average number of hours of sunshine May–October

Braemar 768
Oban 825
Edinburgh 896
Belfast 834
Ambleside 792
Dublin 889
Shannon 893
Scarborough 944
Colwyn Bay 995
Birmingham 875
Kew 1038
Newquay 1089
Bournemouth 1133

RAINFALL

Average annual rainfall
3000 millimetres
2000 millimetres
1000 millimetres
750 millimetres
500 millimetres
→ Prevailing wind

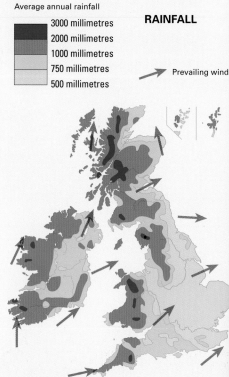

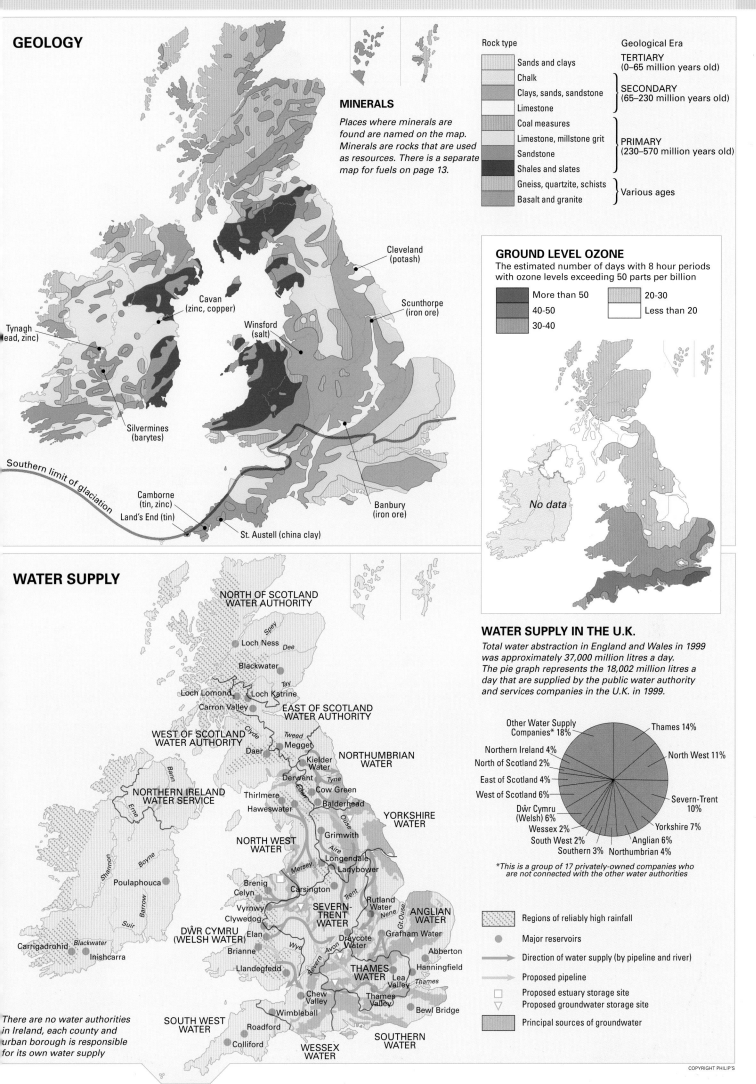

GEOLOGY

MINERALS

Places where minerals are found are named on the map. Minerals are rocks that are used as resources. There is a separate map for fuels on page 13.

Rock type — **Geological Era**

Sands and clays	TERTIARY (0–65 million years old)
Chalk	
Clays, sands, sandstone	SECONDARY (65–230 million years old)
Limestone	
Coal measures	
Limestone, millstone grit	PRIMARY (230–570 million years old)
Sandstone	
Shales and slates	
Gneiss, quartzite, schists	Various ages
Basalt and granite	

Cleveland (potash)

Scunthorpe (iron ore)

Cavan (zinc, copper)

Winsford (salt)

Tynagh (lead, zinc)

Silvermines (barytes)

Southern limit of glaciation

Camborne (tin, zinc)

Land's End (tin)

St. Austell (china clay)

Banbury (iron ore)

GROUND LEVEL OZONE

The estimated number of days with 8 hour periods with ozone levels exceeding 50 parts per billion

More than 50	20-30
40-50	Less than 20
30-40	

No data

WATER SUPPLY

NORTH OF SCOTLAND WATER AUTHORITY

Spey
Loch Ness Dee
Blackwater
Tay
Loch Lomond Loch Katrine
Carron Valley EAST OF SCOTLAND WATER AUTHORITY

WEST OF SCOTLAND WATER AUTHORITY
Clyde Tweed
Daer Megget

NORTHUMBRIAN WATER
Kielder Water
Derwent Tyne
Cow Green
Thirlmere
Haweswater Eden
Balderhead

NORTHERN IRELAND WATER SERVICE
Bann
Erne

Boyne
Shannon

Poulaphouca

YORKSHIRE WATER
Ouse
Grimwith
Aire
Longendale
Mersey Ladybower

NORTH WEST WATER

Barrow
Suir
Carrigadrohid Blackwater
Inishcarra

Brenig
Celyn Carsington
Vyrnwy Trent
Clywedog SEVERN-TRENT WATER Rutland Water
Nene Gt. Ouse
DŴR CYMRU (WELSH WATER) Elan ANGLIAN WATER
Brianne Grafham Water
Wye Draycote Water
Llandegfedd Severn Avon Abberton
THAMES WATER Hanningfield
Chew Valley Lea Valley
Thames Valley Thames
Wimbleball Bewl Bridge
SOUTH WEST WATER Roadford
Colliford SOUTHERN WATER
WESSEX WATER

There are no water authorities in Ireland, each county and urban borough is responsible for its own water supply

WATER SUPPLY IN THE U.K.

Total water abstraction in England and Wales in 1999 was approximately 37,000 million litres a day. The pie graph represents the 18,002 million litres a day that are supplied by the public water authority and services companies in the U.K. in 1999.

Other Water Supply Companies* 18%
Northern Ireland 4%
North of Scotland 2%
East of Scotland 4%
West of Scotland 6%
Dŵr Cymru (Welsh) 6%
Wessex 2%
South West 2%
Southern 3%

Thames 14%
North West 11%
Severn-Trent 10%
Yorkshire 7%
Anglian 6%
Northumbrian 4%

*This is a group of 17 privately-owned companies who are not connected with the other water authorities

	Regions of reliably high rainfall
●	Major reservoirs
→	Direction of water supply (by pipeline and river)
→	Proposed pipeline
□	Proposed estuary storage site
▽	Proposed groundwater storage site
	Principal sources of groundwater

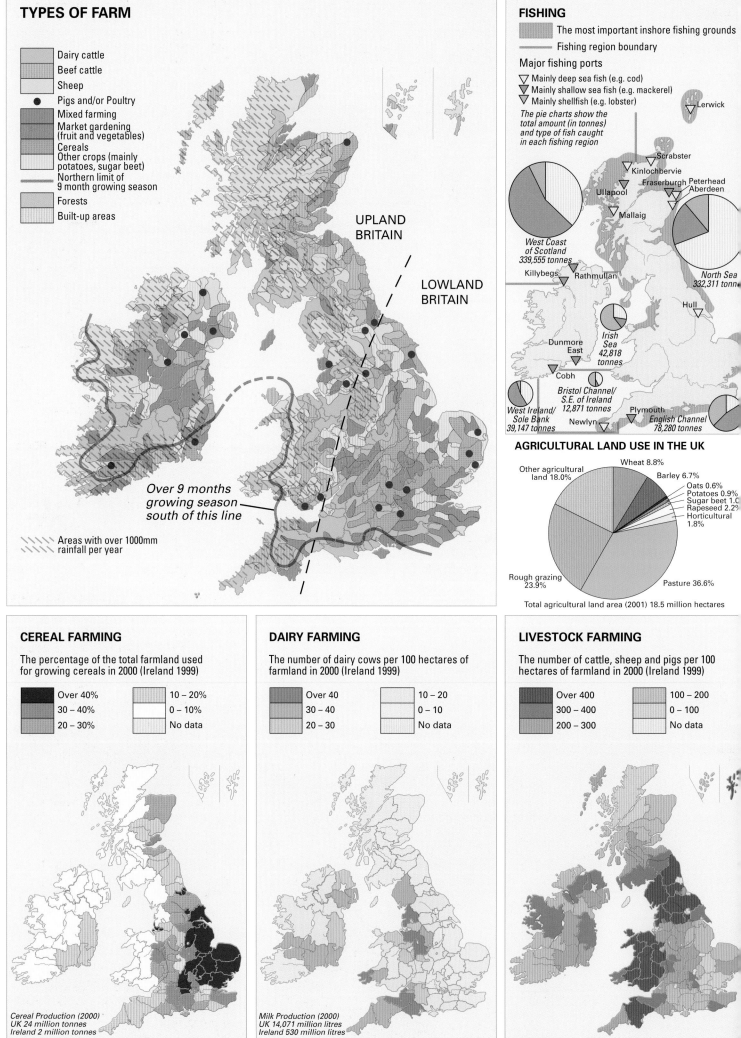

TYPES OF FARM

- Dairy cattle
- Beef cattle
- Sheep
- Pigs and/or Poultry
- Mixed farming
- Market gardening (fruit and vegetables)
- Cereals
- Other crops (mainly potatoes, sugar beet)
- Northern limit of 9 month growing season
- Forests
- Built-up areas

UPLAND BRITAIN

LOWLAND BRITAIN

Over 9 months growing season south of this line

Areas with over 1000mm rainfall per year

FISHING

- The most important inshore fishing grounds
- Fishing region boundary

Major fishing ports
- ▽ Mainly deep sea fish (e.g. cod)
- ▽ Mainly shallow sea fish (e.g. mackerel)
- ▽ Mainly shellfish (e.g. lobster)

The pie charts show the total amount (in tonnes) and type of fish caught in each fishing region

Lerwick

Scrabster
Kinlochbervie
Fraserburgh Peterhead
Aberdeen
Ullapool
Mallaig

West Coast of Scotland 339,555 tonnes

North Sea 332,311 tonnes

Killybegs Rathmullan

Hull

Dunmore East

Irish Sea 42,818 tonnes

Cobh

Bristol Channel/ S.E. of Ireland 12,871 tonnes

West Ireland/ Sole Bank 39,147 tonnes

Newlyn

Plymouth

English Channel 78,280 tonnes

AGRICULTURAL LAND USE IN THE UK

- Other agricultural land 18.0%
- Wheat 8.8%
- Barley 6.7%
- Oats 0.6%
- Potatoes 0.9%
- Sugar beet 1.0
- Rapeseed 2.2%
- Horticultural 1.8%
- Rough grazing 23.9%
- Pasture 36.6%

Total agricultural land area (2001) 18.5 million hectares

CEREAL FARMING

The percentage of the total farmland used for growing cereals in 2000 (Ireland 1999)

- Over 40%
- 30 – 40%
- 20 – 30%
- 10 – 20%
- 0 – 10%
- No data

Cereal Production (2000)
UK 24 million tonnes
Ireland 2 million tonnes

COPYRIGHT PHILIP'S

DAIRY FARMING

The number of dairy cows per 100 hectares of farmland in 2000 (Ireland 1999)

- Over 40
- 30 – 40
- 20 – 30
- 10 – 20
- 0 – 10
- No data

Milk Production (2000)
UK 14,071 million litres
Ireland 530 million litres

LIVESTOCK FARMING

The number of cattle, sheep and pigs per 100 hectares of farmland in 2000 (Ireland 1999)

- Over 400
- 300 – 400
- 200 – 300
- 100 – 200
- 0 – 100
- No data

ENERGY SOURCES

- ▨ Coalfield
- ● Coal-fired* power station (over 1000MW in U.K., over 500MW in Ireland)
- ▨ Peat-cutting area in Ireland
- ◉ Peat-fired* power station (over 100MW)
- △ △ Oilfield
- Oil pipeline (with terminal)
- ○ Oil-fired power station (over 1000MW in U.K., over 500MW in Ireland)
- △ △ Gasfield
- ━● Gas pipeline (with terminal)
- International dividing line
- ▢ UK Sector

- ○ Gas-fired* power station (over 1000MW in U.K., over 500MW in Ireland)
- ○ Combined cycle gas turbine** (over 1000MW)
- ○ Dual-fired power station* (over 1000MW in U.K., over 500MW in Ireland)
- ◉ Hydro-electric power station (over 40MW)
- ○ Pumped storage scheme
- ○ Nuclear power station (over 1000MW)

* Refers to the fuel that is being burnt to generate electricity (in dual-fired stations at least two types of fuel can be burnt, such as coal and oil or oil and gas)

**An efficient use of gas fuel where burnt gas from the main turbine is used to generate steam that is fed to a steam turbine

CHANGES TO COAL MINING IN THE U.K.

	1960	1980	2002
Production (million tonnes)	195	126	32
Number of employees (thousands)	631	297	11
Number of deep mines	698	211	19

U.K. TRADE IN ENERGY 2002

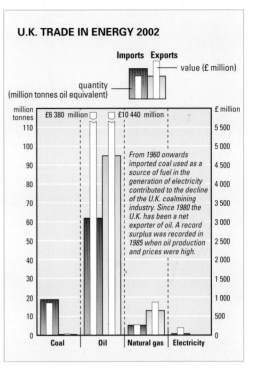

From 1960 onwards imported coal used as a source of fuel in the generation of electricity contributed to the decline of the U.K. coalmining industry. Since 1980 the U.K. has been a net exporter of oil. A record surplus was recorded in 1985 when oil production and prices were high.

ENERGY CONSUMPTION BY FUEL IN THE U.K.

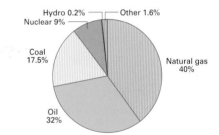

Hydro 0.2% — Other 1.6%
Nuclear 9%
Coal 17.5%
Natural gas 40%
Oil 32%

Total consumption in 2001: 237.7 million tonnes of oil equivalent

ELECTRICITY GENERATION IN THE U.K.

Fuel used in the generation of electricity, 1980 – 2000

- Net imports
- Other fuels
- Hydro-electric
- Nuclear
- Natural gas
- Oil
- Coal

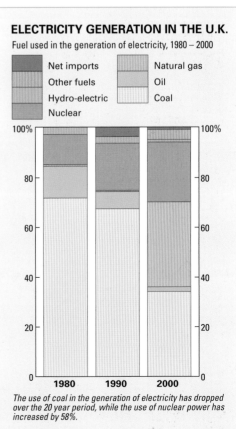

The use of coal in the generation of electricity has dropped over the 20 year period, while the use of nuclear power has increased by 58%.

COPYRIGHT PHILIP'S

Map labels

NORWAY

ATLANTIC OCEAN

Faroe Is.

Shetland Is.

Sullom Voe

Statfjord

Brent

Schiehallion
Foinaven

Orkney Is.

Beryl
Bruce
Harding
Brae
Sleipner

NORWEGIAN SECTOR

Flotta

U.K. SECTOR

Nigg

Fasnakyle
Foyers

Rannoch
Errochty
Clunie
Cruachan
Lochay
Clachan
Sloy
Hunterston

St. Fergus
Peterhead
Cruden Bay

Scott
Britannia
Forties
Nelson

Alba
Andrew
Armada

NORTH SEA

E.T.A.P.

Ekofisk

DANISH SECTOR

U.K. SECTOR

Longannet
Cockenzie
Torness

IRISH SECTOR

Cathaleen's Fall

Ballylumford

Hartlepool

Teesside

DUTCH SECTOR

Barrow in Furness
Heysham

Shannonbridge
Poolbeg

Morecambe
Ferrybridge
Drax
Eggborough
Theddlethorpe
Dimlington & Easington
West Burton

Wylfa
Point of Ayr
Fiddler's Ferry

Viking

Moneypoint
Turlough Hill
Dinorwig
Ffestiniog
Connahs Quay

Ardnacrusha
Tarbert

Ratcliffe-on-Soar

Bacton

Leman

Irish Sea

Rheidol

Aghada

Sizewell

Didcot
Barking
Grain

Kinsale Head

Aberthaw

Kingsnorth
Dungeness

Hinkley Point

Wytch Farm

BELGIUM

Celtic Sea

English Channel

FRANCE

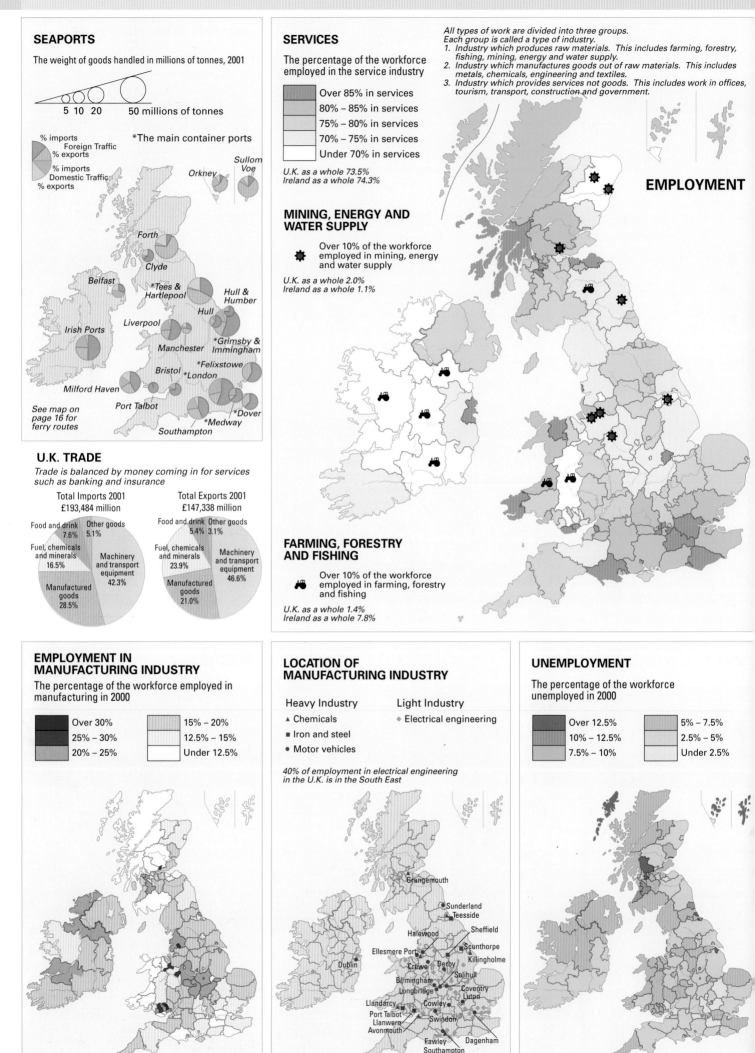

SEAPORTS

The weight of goods handled in millions of tonnes, 2001

5 10 20   50 millions of tonnes

% imports
Foreign Traffic
% exports

% imports
Domestic Traffic
% exports

*The main container ports

Orkney

Sullom Voe

Forth

Clyde

Belfast

*Tees & Hartlepool

Hull & Humber

Hull

Liverpool

Irish Ports

Manchester

*Grimsby & Immingham

Bristol   *Felixstowe
*London

Milford Haven

Port Talbot

*Dover

*Medway

Southampton

See map on page 16 for ferry routes

U.K. TRADE

Trade is balanced by money coming in for services such as banking and insurance

Total Imports 2001
£193,484 million

Food and drink 7.6%
Other goods 5.1%
Fuel, chemicals and minerals 16.5%
Machinery and transport equipment 42.3%
Manufactured goods 28.5%

Total Exports 2001
£147,338 million

Food and drink 5.4%
Other goods 3.1%
Fuel, chemicals and minerals 23.9%
Machinery and transport equipment 46.6%
Manufactured goods 21.0%

SERVICES

The percentage of the workforce employed in the service industry

Over 85% in services
80% – 85% in services
75% – 80% in services
70% – 75% in services
Under 70% in services

U.K. as a whole 73.5%
Ireland as a whole 74.3%

MINING, ENERGY AND WATER SUPPLY

Over 10% of the workforce employed in mining, energy and water supply

U.K. as a whole 2.0%
Ireland as a whole 1.1%

FARMING, FORESTRY AND FISHING

Over 10% of the workforce employed in farming, forestry and fishing

U.K. as a whole 1.4%
Ireland as a whole 7.8%

All types of work are divided into three groups. Each group is called a type of industry.
1. Industry which produces raw materials. This includes farming, forestry, fishing, mining, energy and water supply.
2. Industry which manufactures goods out of raw materials. This includes metals, chemicals, engineering and textiles.
3. Industry which provides services not goods. This includes work in offices, tourism, transport, construction and government.

EMPLOYMENT

EMPLOYMENT IN MANUFACTURING INDUSTRY

The percentage of the workforce employed in manufacturing in 2000

Over 30%
25% – 30%
20% – 25%
15% – 20%
12.5% – 15%
Under 12.5%

LOCATION OF MANUFACTURING INDUSTRY

Heavy Industry
▲ Chemicals
■ Iron and steel
● Motor vehicles

Light Industry
◆ Electrical engineering

40% of employment in electrical engineering in the U.K. is in the South East

Grangemouth
Sunderland
Teesside
Sheffield
Halewood
Scunthorpe
Killingholme
Ellesmere Port
Crewe
Derby
Dublin
Solihull
Birmingham
Coventry
Longbridge
Luton
Llandarcy
Cowley
Port Talbot
Swindon
Llanwern
Avonmouth
Fawley
Dagenham
Southampton

UNEMPLOYMENT

The percentage of the workforce unemployed in 2000

Over 12.5%
10% – 12.5%
7.5% – 10%
5% – 7.5%
2.5% – 5%
Under 2.5%

COPYRIGHT PHILIP'S

POPULATION FACTS

U.K. Population 2001	58,837,000
of which England	49,181,000
Scotland	5,064,000
Wales	2,903,000
N. Ireland	1,689,000
Ireland Population 2001	3,897,000

AGE STRUCTURE OF THE U.K. IN 1901 AND 2001

The age structure shows how old people are and the percentage in each age group that is male and female. The diagram is called a population pyramid. For example, in 1901, 20% of the female population was aged between 10–19. In 2001, about 12% were in this group.

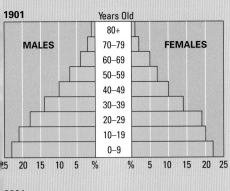

1901

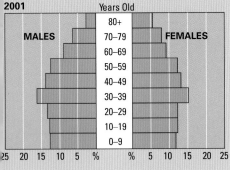

2001

POPULATION DENSITY

Number of people per square kilometre in 2001 (Ireland 2002)

- Over 1000
- 500 – 1000
- 200 – 500
- 100 – 200
- 50 – 100
- 25 – 50
- Under 25

The average density for the U.K. is 243 people per km². The average density for the Republic of Ireland is 57 people per km².

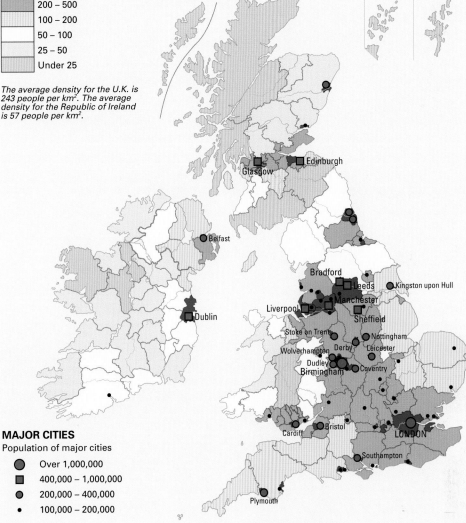

MAJOR CITIES

Population of major cities

- ⬤ Over 1,000,000
- ⬛ 400,000 – 1,000,000
- ● 200,000 – 400,000
- • 100,000 – 200,000

YOUNG PEOPLE

The percentage of the population under 15 years old in 2000 (Ireland 2002)

- Over 22.5%
- 20 – 22.5%
- 19 – 20%
- 18 – 19%
- Under 18%

% young by country
U.K. 20.1%
Ireland 21.1%

OLD PEOPLE

The percentage of the population over pensionable age* in 2000 (Ireland 2002)

- Over 25%
- 20 – 25%
- 17.5 – 20%
- 15 – 17.5%
- 12.5 – 15%
- Under 12.5%

*Pensionable age is 65 for males, 60 for females

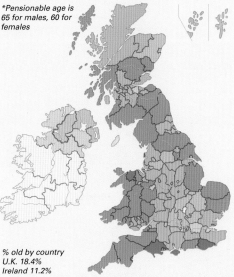

% old by country
U.K. 18.4%
Ireland 11.2%

NATURAL POPULATION CHANGE

The difference between the number of births and the number of deaths per thousand inhabitants in 2000

- Over 7.5 more births
- 5 – 7.5 more births
- 2.5 – 5 more births
- 0 – 2.5 more births
- 0 – 2.5 more deaths
- Over 2.5 more deaths

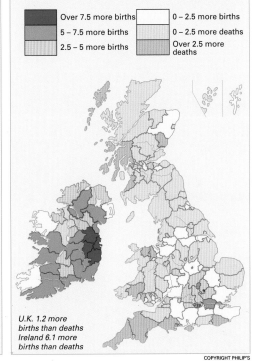

U.K. 1.2 more births than deaths
Ireland 6.1 more births than deaths

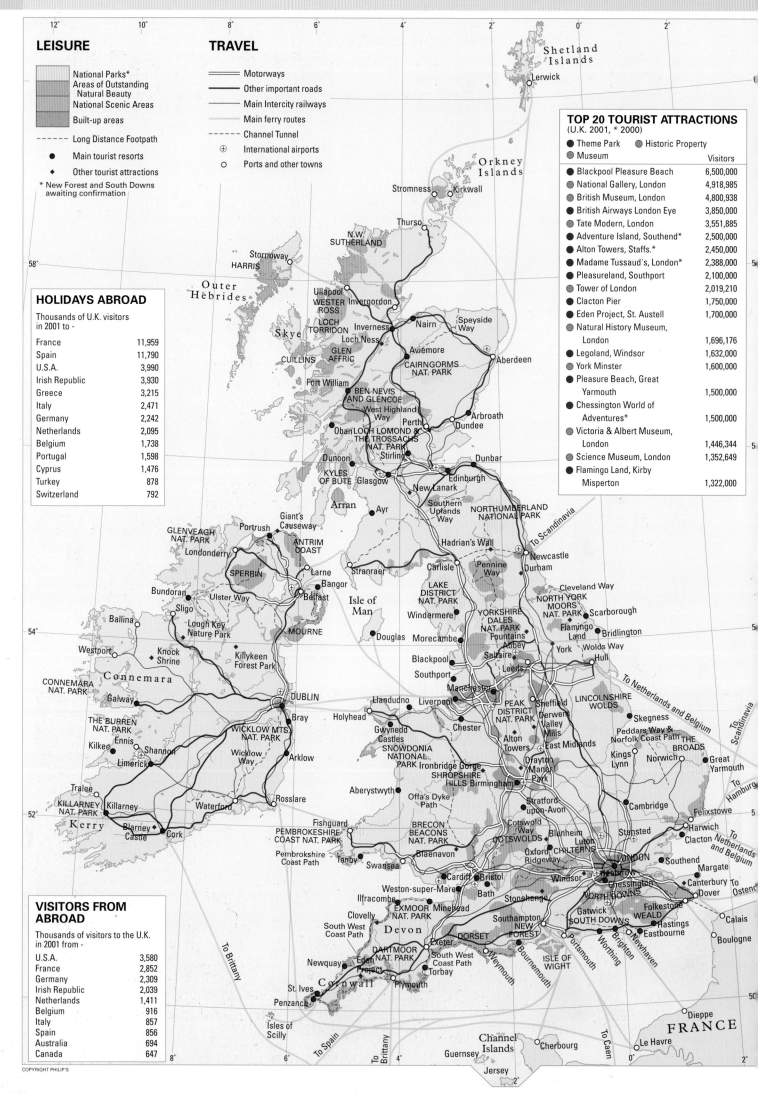

LEISURE

National Parks*
Areas of Outstanding Natural Beauty
National Scenic Areas
Built-up areas

- - - - Long Distance Footpath
● Main tourist resorts
♦ Other tourist attractions

* New Forest and South Downs awaiting confirmation

TRAVEL

══ Motorways
── Other important roads
── Main Intercity railways
── Main ferry routes
- - - - Channel Tunnel
⊕ International airports
○ Ports and other towns

TOP 20 TOURIST ATTRACTIONS
(U.K. 2001, * 2000)

● Theme Park ● Historic Property
● Museum

	Visitors
● Blackpool Pleasure Beach	6,500,000
● National Gallery, London	4,918,985
● British Museum, London	4,800,938
● British Airways London Eye	3,850,000
● Tate Modern, London	3,551,885
● Adventure Island, Southend*	2,500,000
● Alton Towers, Staffs.*	2,450,000
● Madame Tussaud's, London*	2,388,000
● Pleasureland, Southport	2,100,000
● Tower of London	2,019,210
● Clacton Pier	1,750,000
● Eden Project, St. Austell	1,700,000
● Natural History Museum, London	1,696,176
● Legoland, Windsor	1,632,000
● York Minster	1,600,000
● Pleasure Beach, Great Yarmouth	1,500,000
● Chessington World of Adventures*	1,500,000
● Victoria & Albert Museum, London	1,446,344
● Science Museum, London	1,352,649
● Flamingo Land, Kirby Misperton	1,322,000

HOLIDAYS ABROAD

Thousands of U.K. visitors in 2001 to -

France	11,959
Spain	11,790
U.S.A.	3,990
Irish Republic	3,930
Greece	3,215
Italy	2,471
Germany	2,242
Netherlands	2,095
Belgium	1,738
Portugal	1,598
Cyprus	1,476
Turkey	878
Switzerland	792

VISITORS FROM ABROAD

Thousands of visitors to the U.K. in 2001 from -

U.S.A.	3,580
France	2,852
Germany	2,309
Irish Republic	2,039
Netherlands	1,411
Belgium	916
Italy	857
Spain	856
Australia	694
Canada	647

COPYRIGHT PHILIP'S

REGIONAL STUDIES

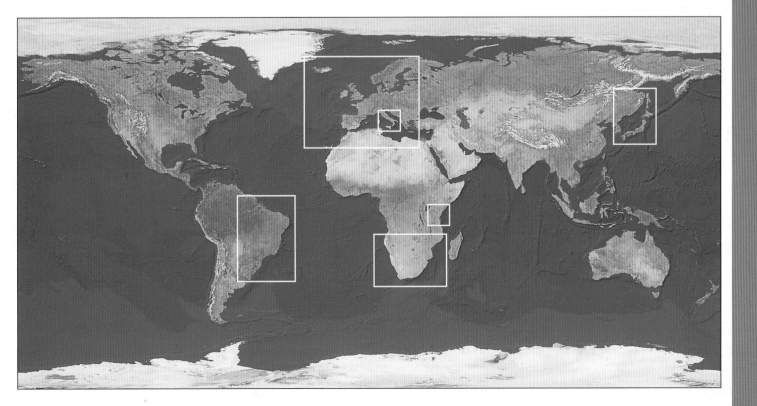

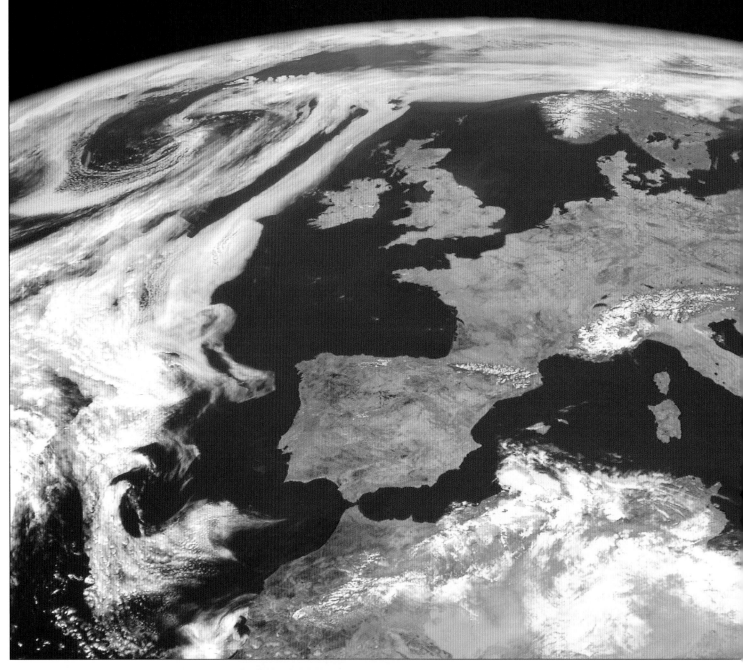

▶ **Netherlands (right)**
Following the construction of the Afluitsdijk Dam across the mouth of the IJsselmeer between 1927 and 1932, large areas of land were drained, forming new fertile land for agriculture. This land, known as *polders*, is seen here in green.

▶ **Naples (far right)**
This image, processed to appear as natural colour, shows Naples on the north side of the bay. To the south-east (lower right) Mount Vesuvius can be seen.

COUNTRIES
Abbreviations

A. = Andorra
BOSNIA-HERZ. = Bosnia-Herzegovina
LI. = Liechtenstein
LUX. = Luxembourg
M. = Monaco
MAC. = Macedonia
S.M. = San Marino
V.C. = Vatican City

Scale 1:37 500 000

| 0 | 300 km | 600 km | 900 km | 1200 km | 1500 km |

1 cm on the map = 375 km on the ground

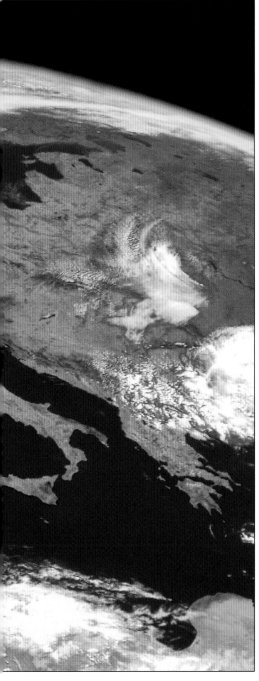

▲ Oblique satellite image of Europe and North Africa

The colours in this European Meteosat satellite image result from the different vegetation and surface temperatures. Europe is largely green, indicating extensive agriculture, and orange from the forests and urban development, while North Africa is mainly brown, indicating the presence of arid desert. A number of weather systems, revealed as white clouds, cover the Atlantic Ocean (left on the image).

Comparing the maps (top, right and overleaf) with the oblique satellite image above will help identify specific countries and land-use types.

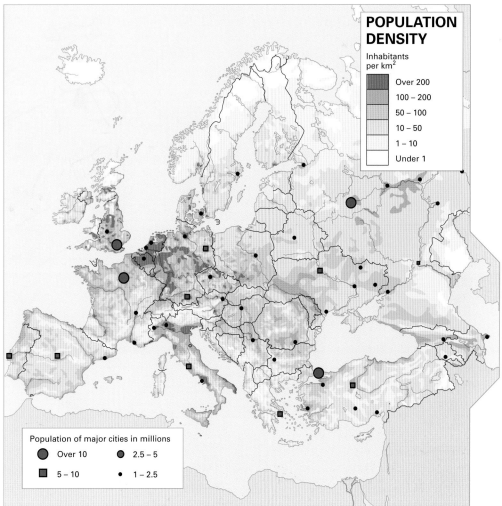

POPULATION DENSITY

Inhabitants per km²

	Over 200
	100 – 200
	50 – 100
	10 – 50
	1 – 10
	Under 1

Population of major cities in millions
- ● Over 10
- ● 2.5 – 5
- ■ 5 – 10
- • 1 – 2.5

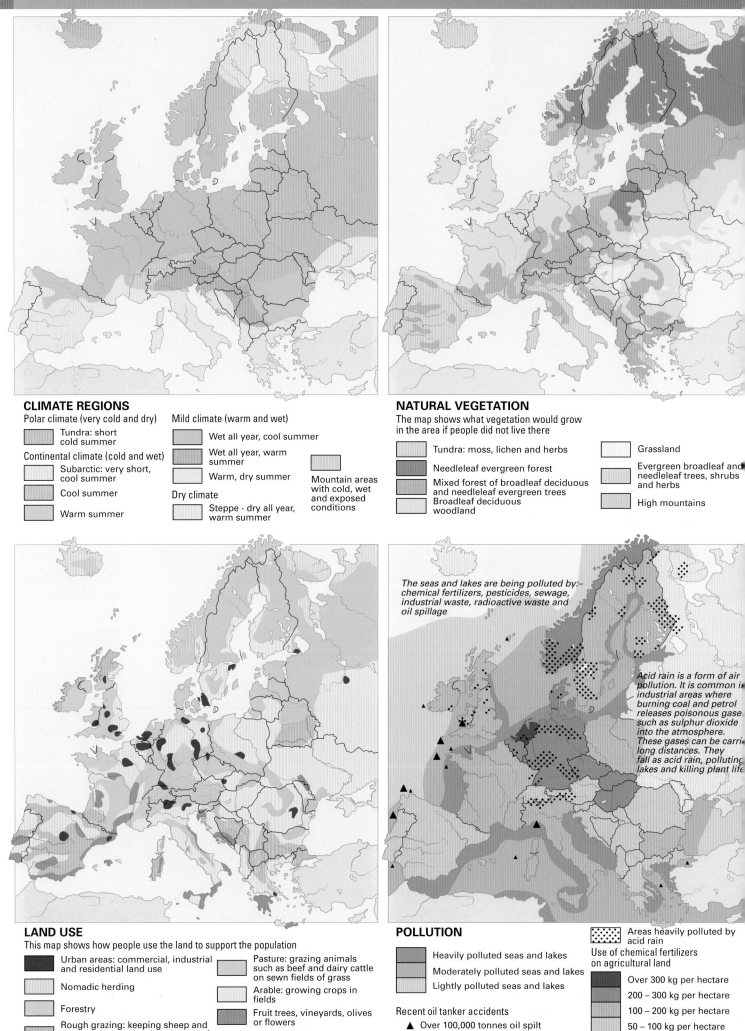

CLIMATE REGIONS

Polar climate (very cold and dry)

Tundra: short cold summer

Continental climate (cold and wet)

Subarctic: very short, cool summer

Cool summer

Warm summer

Mild climate (warm and wet)

Wet all year, cool summer

Wet all year, warm summer

Warm, dry summer

Dry climate

Steppe - dry all year, warm summer

Mountain areas with cold, wet and exposed conditions

NATURAL VEGETATION

The map shows what vegetation would grow in the area if people did not live there

Tundra: moss, lichen and herbs

Needleleaf evergreen forest

Mixed forest of broadleaf deciduous and needleleaf evergreen trees

Broadleaf deciduous woodland

Grassland

Evergreen broadleaf and needleleaf trees, shrubs and herbs

High mountains

LAND USE

This map shows how people use the land to support the population

Urban areas: commercial, industrial and residential land use

Nomadic herding

Forestry

Rough grazing: keeping sheep and goats on large unenclosed areas of natural vegetation

Pasture: grazing animals such as beef and dairy cattle on sewn fields of grass

Arable: growing crops in fields

Fruit trees, vineyards, olives or flowers

Unproductive land

POLLUTION

The seas and lakes are being polluted by:- chemical fertilizers, pesticides, sewage, industrial waste, radioactive waste and oil spillage

Acid rain is a form of air pollution. It is common in industrial areas where burning coal and petrol releases poisonous gases such as sulphur dioxide into the atmosphere. These gases can be carried long distances. They fall as acid rain, polluting lakes and killing plant life

Heavily polluted seas and lakes

Moderately polluted seas and lakes

Lightly polluted seas and lakes

Recent oil tanker accidents

▲ Over 100,000 tonnes oil spilt

▴ 10,000 – 100,000 tonnes oil spilt

Areas heavily polluted by acid rain

Use of chemical fertilizers on agricultural land

Over 300 kg per hectare

200 – 300 kg per hectare

100 – 200 kg per hectare

50 – 100 kg per hectare

Under 50 kg per hectare

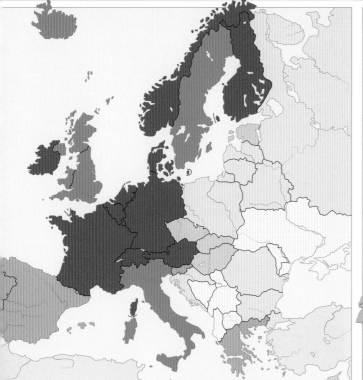

WEALTH

The value of total production divided by population 2001 (US$ per person)

- Over $25,000 per person
- $20 – 25,000 per person
- $15 – 20,000 per person
- $10 – 15,000 per person
- $5 – 10,000 per person
- Under $5,000 per person

Wealthiest countries

Luxembourg $43,400 per person
San Marino $34,600 per person
Switzerland $31,100 per person

Poorest countries

Bosnia-Herz. $1,800 per person
Serbia & Mont. $2,250 per person
Moldova $2,550 per person

EMPLOYMENT

Employment can be divided into three groups: agriculture, industry and services. This map shows the countries with the highest percentage of people in each group

- Over 20% in agriculture (farming, forestry and fishing)
- Over 40% in industry (includes mining and manufacturing)
- Over 60% in services (includes gas, electricity and water supplies, tourism, banking, education)
- Employment is balanced between the groups (under 20% in agriculture, under 40% in industry, under 60% in services)

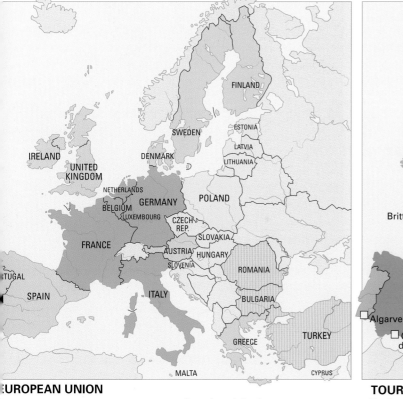

EUROPEAN UNION

- Founder members in 1957

  Belgium, France, Luxembourg, W. Germany, Italy, Netherlands.

- E.U. members at a later date

  U.K., Ireland and Denmark joined in 1973, Greece in 1981, Spain and Portugal in 1986, Austria, Finland and Sweden joined in January 1995.

- Countries admitted to the E.U. in 2004:

  Cyprus, Czech Republic, Estonia, Hungary, Latvia, Lithuania, Malta, Poland, Slovakia and Slovenia.

- Applicant countries to the E.U.

TOURISM

Tourism receipts as a percentage of Gross National Income (G.N.I.), latest available year

- Over 10% of G.N.I. from tourism
- 5–10% of G.N.I. from tourism
- 2.5–5% of G.N.I. from tourism
- 1–2.5% of G.N.I. from tourism
- Under 1% of G.N.I. from tourism

Tourist destinations

- Cultural & historical centres
- Coastal resorts
- Ski resorts
- Centres of entertainment
- Places of pilgrimage
- Places of great natural beauty

COPYRIGHT PHILIP'S

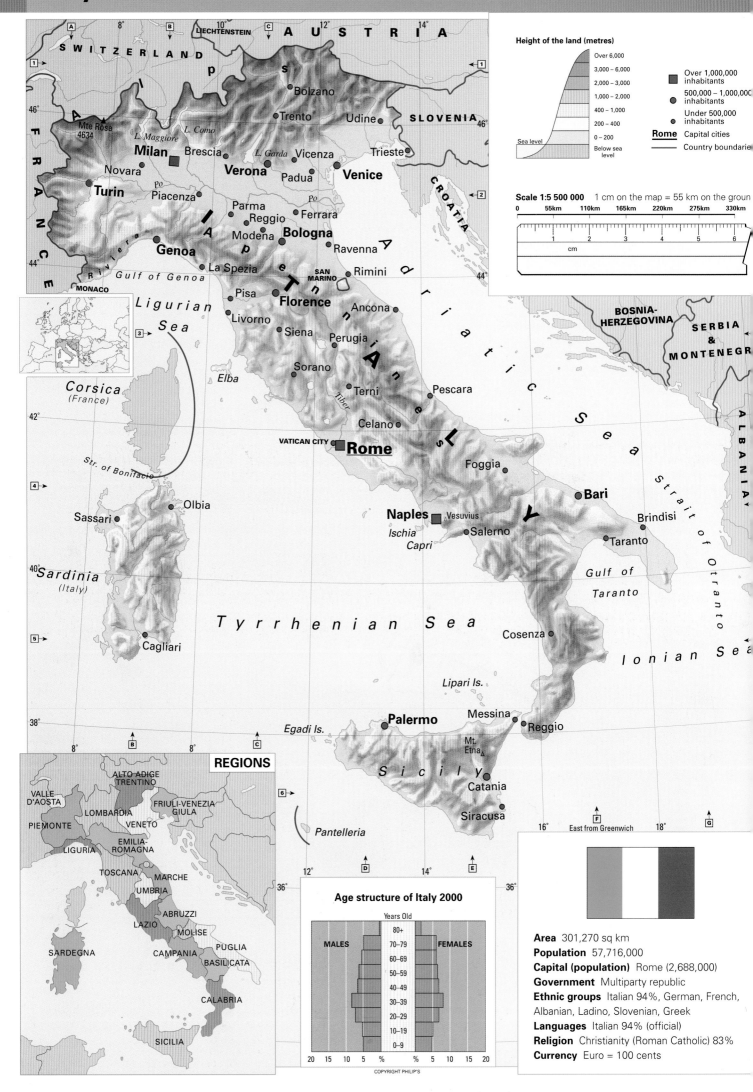

Height of the land (metres)

Over 6,000
3,000 – 6,000
2,000 – 3,000
1,000 – 2,000
400 – 1,000
200 – 400
0 – 200
Sea level
Below sea level

■ Over 1,000,000 inhabitants
● 500,000 – 1,000,000 inhabitants
● Under 500,000 inhabitants

Rome Capital cities
— Country boundaries

Scale 1:5 500 000   1 cm on the map = 55 km on the ground

0   55km 110km 165km 220km 275km 330km

cm

REGIONS

VALLE D'AOSTA
PIEMONTE
LOMBARDIA
ALTO ADIGE TRENTINO
FRIULI-VENEZIA GIULA
VENETO
LIGURIA
EMILIA-ROMAGNA
TOSCANA
MARCHE
UMBRIA
ABRUZZI
LAZIO
MOLISE
SARDEGNA
CAMPANIA
PUGLIA
BASILICATA
CALABRIA
SICILIA

Age structure of Italy 2000

Years Old

MALES   FEMALES

80+
70–79
60–69
50–59
40–49
30–39
20–29
10–19
0–9

20 15 10   5   %   %   5 10 15 20

COPYRIGHT PHILIP'S

Area 301,270 sq km
Population 57,716,000
Capital (population) Rome (2,688,000)
Government Multiparty republic
Ethnic groups Italian 94%, German, French, Albanian, Ladino, Slovenian, Greek
Languages Italian 94% (official)
Religion Christianity (Roman Catholic) 83%
Currency Euro = 100 cents

INDUSTRY

The percentage
of the workforce
employed in
industry 2001

	Over 40%
	35 – 40%
	30 – 35%
	25 – 30%
	20 – 25%
	Under 20%

OUT OF WORK

The percentage of
the workforce
unemployed in 2001

	Over 20%
	16 – 20%
	12 – 16%
	10 – 12%
	8 – 10%
	6 – 8%
	Under 6%

Unemployment rate
for people
under 25 years old

■	Over 30%
■	20 – 30%
•	Under 20%

▲ Italy

At the centre of the image lies Italy, with the
island of Sicily at its base. The Alps are identified
in white and green to the north of Italy, and to
the west of the Tyrrhenian Sea are the islands
of Corsica and Sardinia. Albania and the former
Yugoslav republics of Slovenia, Croatia and
Bosnia-Herzegovina are to be seen to the east
across the Adriatic Sea.

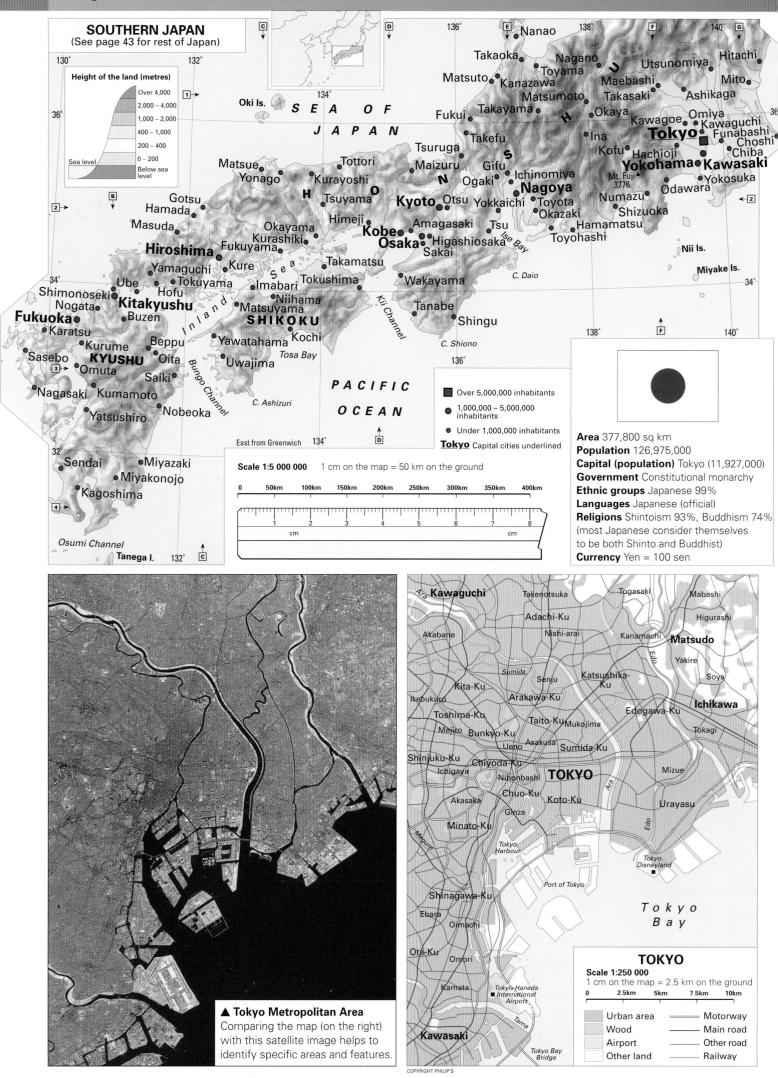

SOUTHERN JAPAN
(See page 43 for rest of Japan)

Height of the land (metres)

Over 4,000
2,000 – 4,000
1,000 – 2,000
400 – 1,000
200 – 400
0 – 200
Below sea level
Sea level

SEA OF JAPAN

Oki Is.

Nanao
Takaoka
Nagano
Utsunomiya
Hitachi
Toyama
Matsuto
Kanazawa
Maebashi
Mito
Matsumoto
Takasaki
Ashikaga
Fukui
Takayama
Okaya
Kawagoe
Omiya
Kawaguchi
Takefu
Ina
Kofu
Tokyo
Funabashi
Choshi
Tsuruga
Maizuru
Gifu
Ichinomiya
Hachioji
Chiba
Matsue
Tottori
Kyoto
Ogaki
Mt. Fuji
Yokohama
Kawasaki
Yonago
Kurayoshi
Otsu
Yokkaichi
3776
Yokosuka
Tsuyama
Nagoya
Numazu
Odawara
Himeji
Toyota
Okazaki
Hamada
Okayama
Tsu
Shizuoka
Masuda
Kurashiki
Amagasaki
Kobe
Hamamatsu
Hiroshima
Fukuyama
Osaka
Higashiosaka
Toyohashi
Ise Bay
Nii Is.
Yamaguchi
Kure
Sakai
C. Daio
Ube
Tokuyama
Imabari
Takamatsu
Miyake Is.
Shimonoseki
Hofu
Niihama
Tokushima
Nogata
Kitakyushu
Matsuyama
SHIKOKU
Kochi
Wakayama
Fukuoka
Buzen
Yawatahama
Tanabe
Karatsu
Beppu
Uwajima
Shingu
Kurume
Oita
KYUSHU
Sasebo
Omuta
Saiki
C. Shiono
Nagasaki
Kumamoto
Nobeoka
PACIFIC OCEAN
Yatsushiro
C. Ashizuri
Sendai
Miyazaki
Miyakonojo
Kagoshima
Osumi Channel
Tanega I.

Inland Sea
Tosa Bay
Kii Channel
Bungo Channel

East from Greenwich

■ Over 5,000,000 inhabitants
● 1,000,000 – 5,000,000 inhabitants
• Under 1,000,000 inhabitants
Tokyo Capital cities underlined

Scale 1:5 000 000   1 cm on the map = 50 km on the ground

0   50km 100km 150km 200km 250km 300km 350km 400km

cm   1   2   3   4   5   6   7   8   cm

Area 377,800 sq km
Population 126,975,000
Capital (population) Tokyo (11,927,000)
Government Constitutional monarchy
Ethnic groups Japanese 99%
Languages Japanese (official)
Religions Shintoism 93%, Buddhism 74% (most Japanese consider themselves to be both Shinto and Buddhist)
Currency Yen = 100 sen

▲ Tokyo Metropolitan Area
Comparing the map (on the right) with this satellite image helps to identify specific areas and features.

Kawaguchi
Ara
Takenotsuka
Togasaki
Mabashi
Adachi-Ku
Nishi-arai
Higurashi
Akabane
Kanamachi
Matsudo
Edo
Yakire
Sumida
Senju
Katsushika-Ku
Soya
Kita-Ku
Arakawa-Ku
Ikebukuro
Ichikawa
Toshima-Ku
Taito-Ku
Edogawa-Ku
Mejiro
Bunkyo-Ku
Mukojima
Tokagi
Shinjuku-Ku
Ueno
Asakusa
Sumida-Ku
Mizue
Ichigaya
Chiyoda-Ku
Nihonbashi
TOKYO
Akasaka
Chuo-Ku
Koto-Ku
Urayasu
Ginza
Minato-Ku
Ara
Meguro
Tokyo Harbour
Tokyo Disneyland
Shinagawa-Ku
Port of Tokyo
Ebara
Tokyo Bay
Oimachi
Ota-Ku
Omori
Edo
Kamata
Tokyo-Haneda International Airport
Tama
Tokyo Bay Bridge
Kawasaki

TOKYO
Scale 1:250 000
1 cm on the map = 2.5 km on the ground
0   2.5km   5km   7.5km   10km

Urban area
Wood
Airport
Other land

Motorway
Main road
Other road
Railway

COPYRIGHT PHILIP'S

VOLCANOES AND EARTHQUAKES

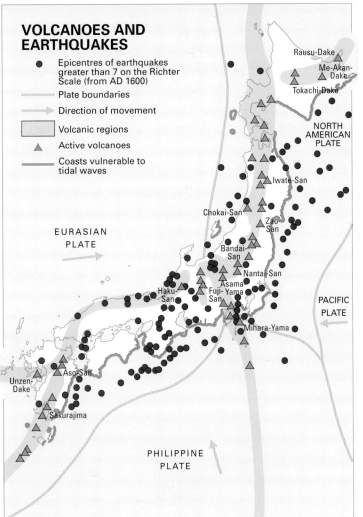

- ● Epicentres of earthquakes greater than 7 on the Richter Scale (from AD 1600)
- ░ Plate boundaries
- ⇨ Direction of movement
- ▨ Volcanic regions
- ▲ Active volcanoes
- ━ Coasts vulnerable to tidal waves

EURASIAN PLATE

NORTH AMERICAN PLATE

PACIFIC PLATE

PHILIPPINE PLATE

Rausu-Dake
Me-Akan-Dake
Tokachi-Dake
Iwate-San
Chokai-San
Zao-San
Bandai-San
Nantai-San
Asama
Haku-San
Fuji-Yama
San
Mihara-Yama
Aso-San
Unzen-Dake
Sakurajima

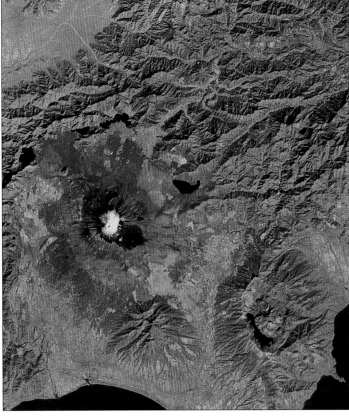

▲ Mount Fuji, Japan
The white snow-capped feature, just below the centre of the picture, is Mount Fuji. The cone is seen as dark green, with a black deposit of ash from its 1707 eruption. The volcano is 3,776 metres high and 30 kilometres wide across its base.

POPULATION

The number of people per square kilometre

- ▨ Over 400
- ▨ 300 – 400
- ▨ 200 – 300
- ▨ 100 – 300
- ☐ Under 100

Population of major cities

- ■ Over 2,000,000
- ● 1,000,000 – 2,000,000
- ● 500,000 – 1,000,000
- • 250,000 – 500,000

Cities with populations over one million are named on the map

Sapporo
Kawasaki
Tokyo
Kyoto
Nagoya
Kobe
Yokohama
Hiroshima
Osaka
Kitakyushu
Fukuoka

Age structure of Japan 2000

Years Old
MALES | FEMALES
80+
70–79
60–69
50–59
40–49
30–39
20–29
10–19
0–9
20 15 10 5 %   % 5 10 15 20

INDUSTRY

- ● Iron and steel
- ☐ Motor vehicles
- ▲ Electrical engineering
- ▽ Textiles
- ★ Chemicals

The percentage of the workforce employed in manufacturing

- ▨ Over 30%
- ▨ 25% – 30%
- ▨ 20% – 25%
- ▨ 15% – 20%
- ☐ Under 15%

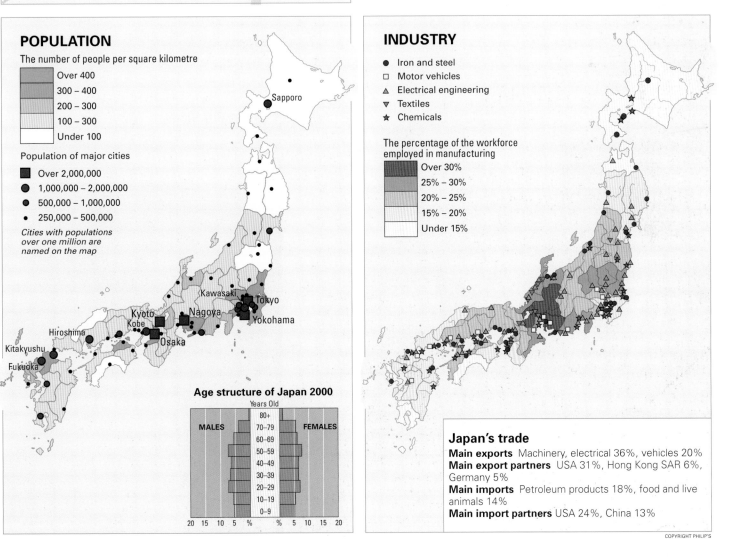

Japan's trade

Main exports Machinery, electrical 36%, vehicles 20%
Main export partners USA 31%, Hong Kong SAR 6%, Germany 5%
Main imports Petroleum products 18%, food and live animals 14%
Main import partners USA 24%, China 13%

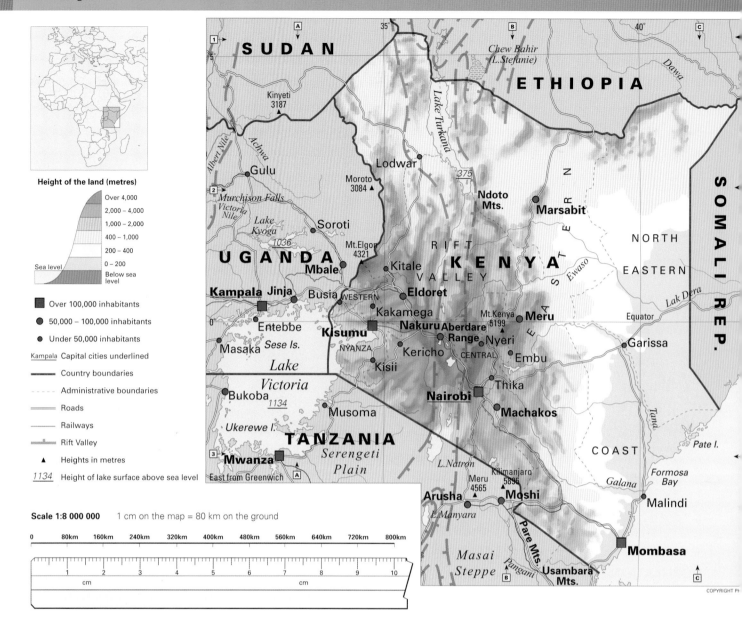

Height of the land (metres)

- Over 4,000
- 2,000 – 4,000
- 1,000 – 2,000
- 400 – 1,000
- 200 – 400
- 0 – 200
- Below sea level

Sea level

■ Over 100,000 inhabitants
● 50,000 – 100,000 inhabitants
• Under 50,000 inhabitants

Kampala Capital cities underlined

━━━ Country boundaries
----- Administrative boundaries
═══ Roads
─── Railways
═══ Rift Valley
▲ Heights in metres
1134 Height of lake surface above sea level

Scale 1:8 000 000   1 cm on the map = 80 km on the ground

| 0 | 80km | 160km | 240km | 320km | 400km | 480km | 560km | 640km | 720km | 800km |

Great Rift Valley

▼ Great Rift Valley

The infrared satellite image below shows vegetation in red, water in blue/black and bare ground and buildings in light blue.

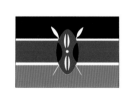

Area 580,370 sq km
Population 31,139,000
Capital (Population) Nairobi (2,000,000)
Government Multiparty republic
Ethnic groups Kikuyu 21%, Luhya 14%, Luo 13%, Kamba 11%, Kalenjin 11%
Languages Swahili and English (both official)
Religions Christianity (Roman Catholic 27%, Protestant 19%, others 27%), traditional beliefs 19%, Islam 6%
Currency Kenya shilling = 100 cents

Exports

Kenya total exports 2000, US$ 1,571 million

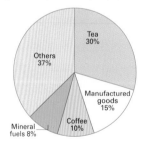

- Tea 30%
- Others 37%
- Manufactured goods 15%
- Coffee 10%
- Mineral fuels 8%

Imports

Kenya total imports 2000, US$ 2,891 million

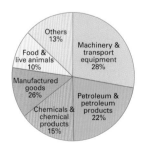

- Others 13%
- Machinery & transport equipment 28%
- Food & live animals 10%
- Manufactured goods 26%
- Petroleum & petroleum products 22%
- Chemicals & chemical products 15%

Age structure of Kenya 2000

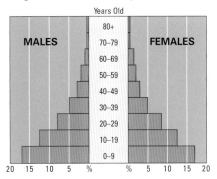

Years Old

MALES		FEMALES

80+
70–79
60–69
50–59
40–49
30–39
20–29
10–19
0–9

20 15 10 5   %   % 5 10 15 20

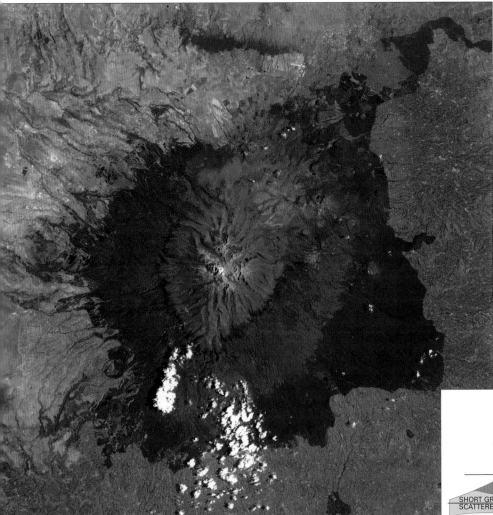

◀ Mount Kenya

The satellite used to acquire this image orbited at around 700 kilometres above the Earth's surface. The dark green in the satellite image represents coniferous forest, while the lighter green indicates deciduous forest. Mount Kenya is 5,199 metres high, the second highest mountain in Africa, after Mount Kilimanjaro, Tanzania.

Changes in vegetation with Mount Kenya

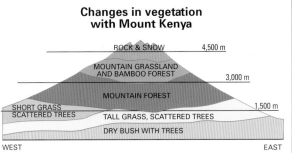

ROCK & SNOW   4,500 m
MOUNTAIN GRASSLAND AND BAMBOO FOREST   3,000 m
MOUNTAIN FOREST
SHORT GRASS SCATTERED TREES   1,500 m
TALL GRASS, SCATTERED TREES
DRY BUSH WITH TREES

WEST   EAST

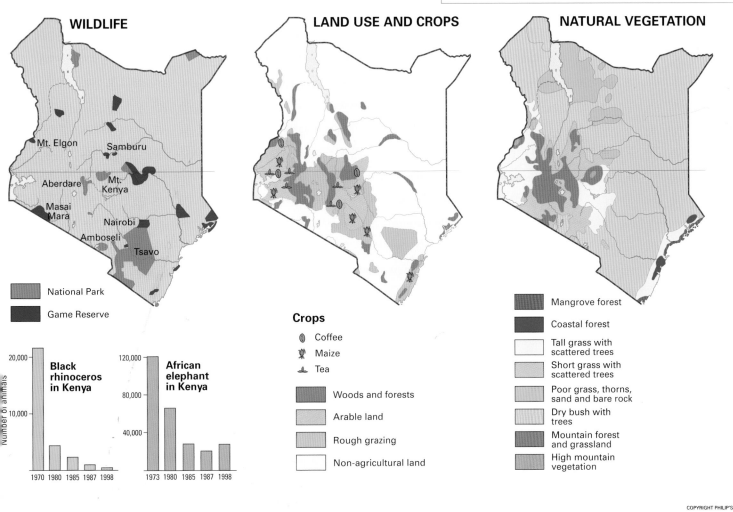

WILDLIFE

Mt. Elgon
Samburu
Aberdare
Mt. Kenya
Masai Mara
Nairobi
Amboseli
Tsavo

■ National Park
■ Game Reserve

Black rhinoceros in Kenya

20,000
10,000

1970 1980 1985 1987 1998

Number of animals

African elephant in Kenya

120,000
80,000
40,000

1973 1980 1985 1987 1998

LAND USE AND CROPS

Crops

⦿ Coffee
🌿 Maize
🌿 Tea

■ Woods and forests
■ Arable land
■ Rough grazing
□ Non-agricultural land

NATURAL VEGETATION

■ Mangrove forest
■ Coastal forest
□ Tall grass with scattered trees
■ Short grass with scattered trees
■ Poor grass, thorns, sand and bare rock
■ Dry bush with trees
■ Mountain forest and grassland
■ High mountain vegetation

COPYRIGHT PHILIP'S

▶ **Cape of Good Hope, South Africa**

This satellite image shows the area around the Cape Peninsula in South Africa, stretching south-eastwards towards Cape Agulhas. Cape Town lies near the top of the peninsula (at the far left), while the Cape of Good Hope is shown at the bottom. The dark area on the coast next to Cape Town is Table Mountain.

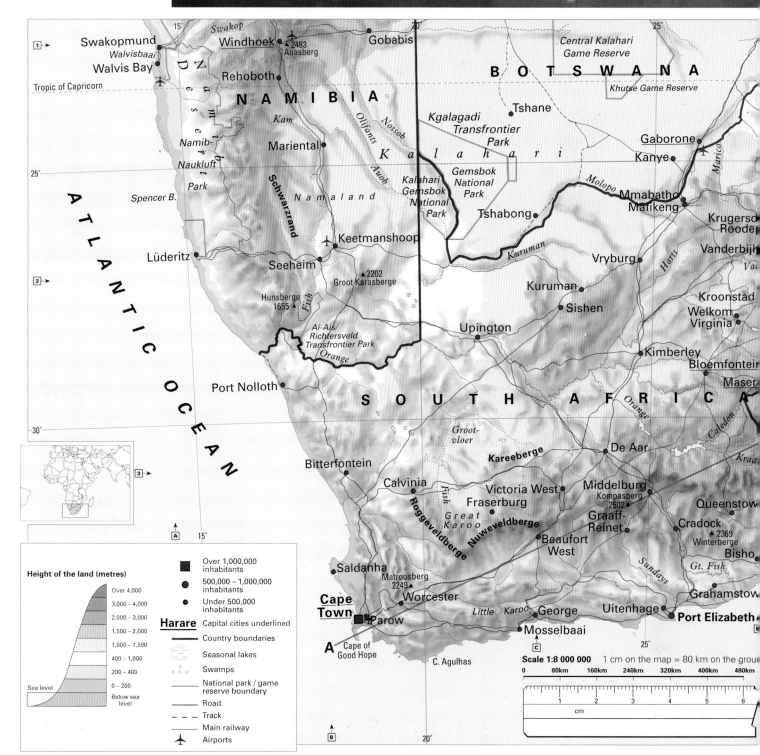

Height of the land (metres)

Over 4,000	
3,000 – 4,000	
2,000 – 3,000	
1,500 – 2,000	
1,000 – 1,500	
400 – 1,000	
200 – 400	
0 – 200	
Sea level	
	Below sea level

■ Over 1,000,000 inhabitants
● 500,000 – 1,000,000 inhabitants
• Under 500,000 inhabitants

Harare Capital cities underlined

Country boundaries
Seasonal lakes
Swamps
National park / game reserve boundary
Road
Track
Main railway
✈ Airports

Scale 1:8 000 000   1 cm on the map = 80 km on the ground

0   80km   160km   240km   320km   400km   480km

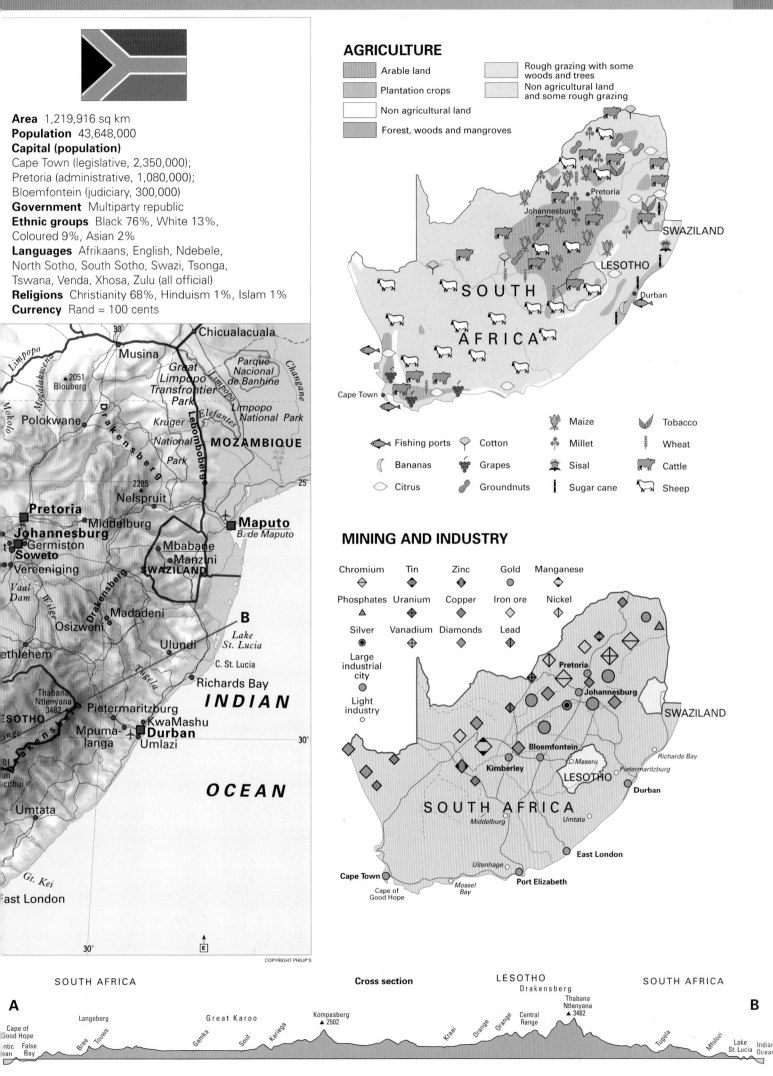

Area 1,219,916 sq km
Population 43,648,000
Capital (population)
Cape Town (legislative, 2,350,000);
Pretoria (administrative, 1,080,000);
Bloemfontein (judiciary, 300,000)
Government Multiparty republic
Ethnic groups Black 76%, White 13%,
Coloured 9%, Asian 2%
Languages Afrikaans, English, Ndebele,
North Sotho, South Sotho, Swazi, Tsonga,
Tswana, Venda, Xhosa, Zulu (all official)
Religions Christianity 68%, Hinduism 1%, Islam 1%
Currency Rand = 100 cents

AGRICULTURE

Arable land
Plantation crops
Non agricultural land
Forest, woods and mangroves
Rough grazing with some woods and trees
Non agricultural land and some rough grazing

Fishing ports
Bananas
Citrus
Cotton
Grapes
Groundnuts
Maize
Millet
Sisal
Sugar cane
Tobacco
Wheat
Cattle
Sheep

MINING AND INDUSTRY

Chromium
Phosphates
Silver
Large industrial city
Light industry
Tin
Uranium
Vanadium
Zinc
Copper
Diamonds
Gold
Iron ore
Lead
Manganese
Nickel

Pretoria
Johannesburg
Bloemfontein
Kimberley
Maseru
LESOTHO
Maseru
Richards Bay
Pietermaritzburg
Durban
SOUTH AFRICA
Middelburg
Umtata
East London
Cape Town
Uitenhage
Mossel Bay
Port Elizabeth
Cape of Good Hope
SWAZILAND

COPYRIGHT PHILIP'S

SOUTH AFRICA
Cross section
LESOTHO
Drakensberg
SOUTH AFRICA

A
Langeberg
Great Karoo
Kompasberg ▲ 2502
Thabana Ntlenyana ▲ 3482
Central Range
B

Cape of Good Hope
Atlantic Ocean
False Bay
Bree
Touws
Gamka
Sout
Kariega
Kraai
Orange
Orange
Tugela
Mfolozi
Lake St. Lucia
Indian Ocean

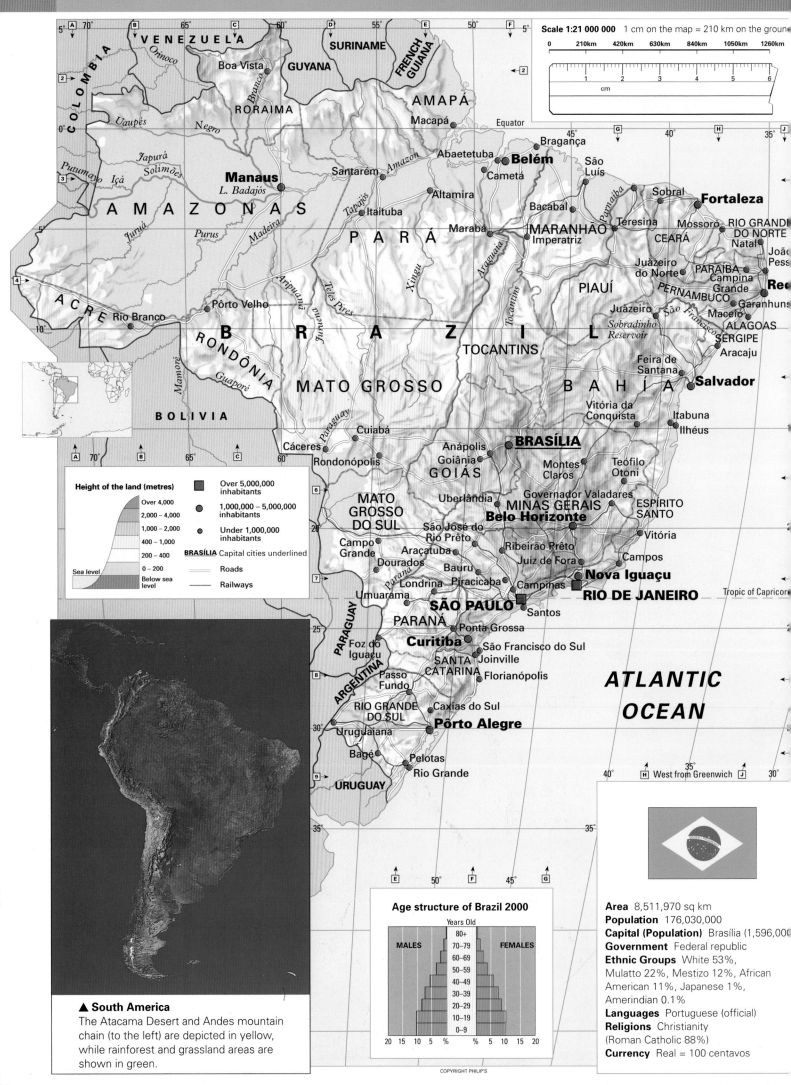

Scale 1:21 000 000 1 cm on the map = 210 km on the ground

0 210km 420km 630km 840km 1050km 1260km

Height of the land (metres)

Over 4,000
2,000 – 4,000
1,000 – 2,000
400 – 1,000
200 – 400
0 – 200
Sea level
Below sea level

Over 5,000,000 inhabitants
1,000,000 – 5,000,000 inhabitants
Under 1,000,000 inhabitants
BRASÍLIA Capital cities underlined
Roads
Railways

▲ South America
The Atacama Desert and Andes mountain chain (to the left) are depicted in yellow, while rainforest and grassland areas are shown in green.

Age structure of Brazil 2000

Years Old

MALES | FEMALES
80+
70–79
60–69
50–59
40–49
30–39
20–29
10–19
0–9

20 15 10 5 % 5 10 15 20

Area 8,511,970 sq km
Population 176,030,000
Capital (Population) Brasília (1,596,000)
Government Federal republic
Ethnic Groups White 53%, Mulatto 22%, Mestizo 12%, African American 11%, Japanese 1%, Amerindian 0.1%
Languages Portuguese (official)
Religions Christianity (Roman Catholic 88%)
Currency Real = 100 centavos

COPYRIGHT PHILIP'S

MINING

Chromium	Tin	Zinc	Gold
Bauxite	Copper	Iron ore	Manganese
	Coal	Oil	

Exports

Brazil total exports 2001 US$58,223 million

Others

Machinery 26.7% (of which motor vehicles 7.4%)

Manufactured goods 17.8% (of which iron and steel 5.5%)

Food & live animals 20.0% (of which coffee 2.4%)

Crude materials 15.0% (of which iron ore 5.0%)

Fuel 3.6%

Chemicals 5.4%

Imports

Brazil total imports 2001 US$58,510 million

Others

Machinery 43.0% (of which motor vehicles 6.7%)

Food & live animals 5.0%

Crude materials 2.6%

Fuel 14.5%

Chemicals 18.0%

Manufactured goods 9.9% (of which textiles 1.7%)

AGRICULTURE AND INDUSTRY

- Industrial
- Arable land
- Plantation crops
- Pasture
- Forest, woods and mangroves
- Rough grazing

Fishing ports	Cotton	Tea
Bananas	Groundnuts	Tobacco
Cacao	Maize	Cattle
Citrus fruit	Potatoes	Pigs
Coconuts	Rice	
Coffee	Sugar cane	

Fortaleza

Recife

Salvador

Brasília

Belo Horizonte

São Paulo

Rio de Janeiro

Pôrto Alegre

DEFORESTATION

▶ **Deforestation in Brazil**

False colours have been chosen to highlight the destruction of the rainforest. The dark green of the natural forest contrasts with the pinks of levelled forest, within a typical, linear, branching pattern of destruction.

Average annual change in forest cover (selected countries in thousand hectares, 1990–2000). Loss as a percentage of remaining stocks is shown in figures on each column.

Country	Value (thousand hectares)	Loss %
Brazil	2,300	0.4
Indonesia	1,300	1.2
Sudan	960	1.4
Mexico	630	1.1
Dem. Rep. of Congo	530	0.4
Burma	510	1.4
Nigeria	400	2.6
Argentina	280	0.8
Australia	270	0.2
Peru	260	0.4
Ivory Coast	270	3.1
Malaysia	230	1.2
Cameroon	220	0.9
Ecuador	140	1.2
Ghana	120	1.7
Botswana	120	0.9
Madagascar	120	0.9

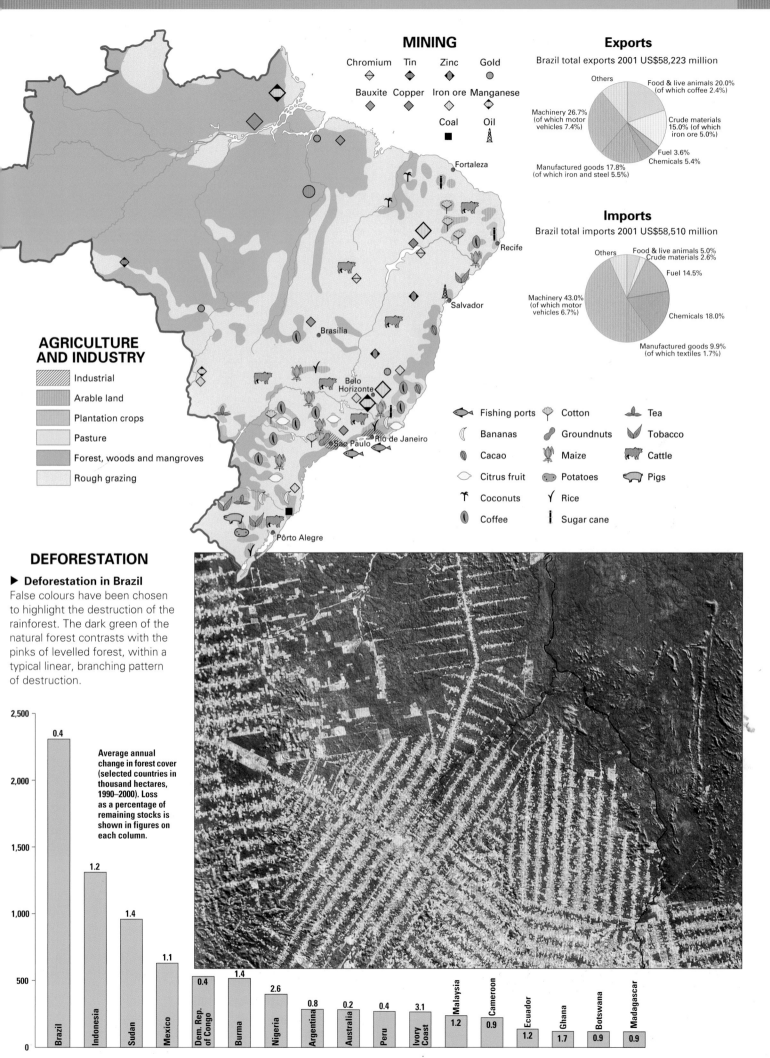

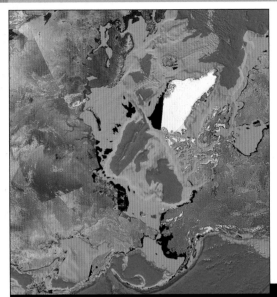

◀ Arctic Ocean
This image is coloured green for ocean depths down to 3,000 metres and blue for depths greater than 3,000 metres.

▶ Northern hemisphere 'ozone hole', March 2000
The colours represent the ozone concentration in Dobson Units. The ozone hole is visible at the centre of the image. Ozone depletion is caused by CFCs, a group of manufactured chemicals used in air-conditioning systems and refrigerators.

▲ Antarctica
The colours on this satellite mosaic have been enhanced to reveal the large-scale structure of the ice cover over the continent. Most of the ice shown here covers land, with the exception of the Ross Ice Shelf (brown tint, lower left of centre) and the Ronne Ice Shelf (brown tint, left of centre). The permanent ice cover is over 3,000 metres thick near the centre of the continent, and covers a total area of over 12.5 million square kilometres.

◀ Antarctic 'ozone hole', September 2000
This false-colour image shows the total atmospheric ozone concentration in the southern hemisphere. The ozone hole can be clearly seen at the centre, over Antarctica.

THE WORLD

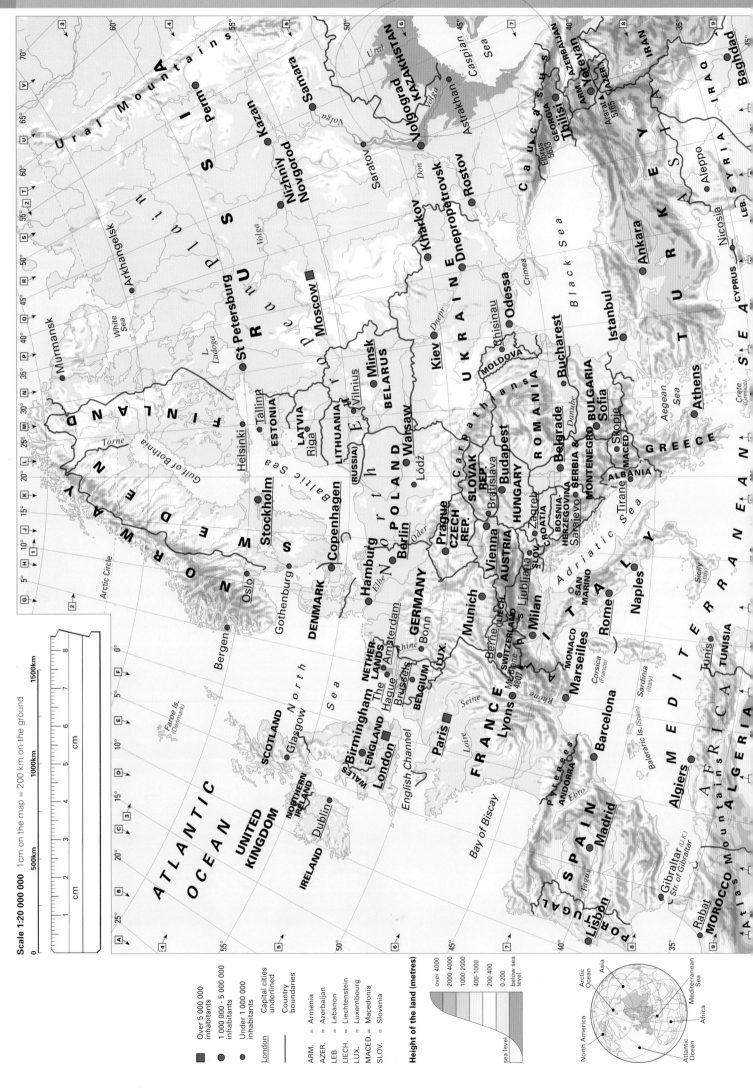

Scale 1:20 000 000 1cm on the map = 200 km on the ground

1500km
1000km
500km

Over 5 000 000 inhabitants

1 000 000 – 5 000 000 inhabitants

Under 1 000 000 inhabitants

London Capital cities underlined

Country boundaries

ARM. = Armenia
AZER. = Azerbaijan
LEB. = Lebanon
LIECH. = Liechtenstein
LUX. = Luxembourg
MACED. = Macedonia
SLOV. = Slovenia

Height of the land (metres)

over 4000
2000-4000
1000-2000
400-1000
200-400
0-200
below sea level

sea level

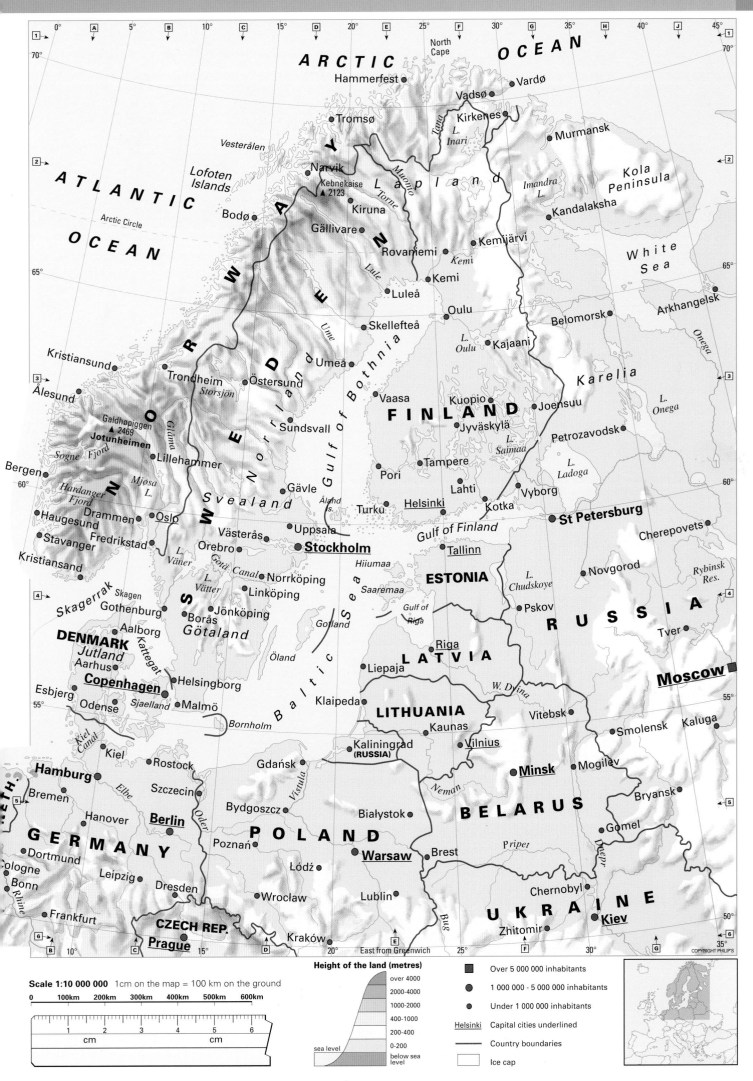

ARCTIC OCEAN

North Cape

Hammerfest
Vardø
Vadsø
Kirkenes
L. Inari
Tromsø
Murmansk
Vesterålen
Lapland
Imandra L.
Kola Peninsula
Lofoten Islands
Narvik
Kandalaksha
Kebnekaise ▲ 2123
Bodø
Kiruna
Arctic Circle
Gällivare
Kemijärvi
Rovaniemi
Kemi
White Sea
Kristiansund
Trondheim
Östersund
Skellefteå
Belomorsk
Arkhangelsk
Ålesund
Storsjön
Umeå
L. Oulu
Kajaani
Karelia
Galdhøpiggen ▲ 2469
Jotunheimen
Lillehammer
Sundsvall
Vaasa
Kuopio
Joensuu
Petrozavodsk
L. Onega
Bergen
Mjøsa L.
Gävle
FINLAND
Jyväskylä
Hardanger Fjord
Drammen
Oslo
Åland Is.
Turku
Pori
Tampere
Lahti
L. Saimaa
L. Ladoga
Sogne Fjord
Haugesund
Fredrikstad
Västerås
Uppsala
Helsinki
Kotka
Vyborg
Stavanger
Örebro
Stockholm
Gulf of Finland
St Petersburg
Cherepovets
Kristiansand
L. Väner
Götä Canal
Norrköping
Tallinn
Hiiumaa
Novgorod
Rybinsk Res.
Skagerrak
Skagen
Gothenburg
Borås
L. Vätter
Linköping
ESTONIA
Saaremaa
Gulf of Riga
L. Chudskoye
Pskov
Tver
DENMARK
Jutland
Aalborg
Jönköping
Götaland
Gotland
Öland
RUSSIA
Aarhus
Helsingborg
Riga
Copenhagen
Odense
Sjaelland
Malmö
LATVIA
Liepaja
Moscow
Esbjerg
Bornholm
W. Dvina
Kiel Canal
Kiel
Klaipeda
LITHUANIA
Vitebsk
Smolensk
Kaluga
Hamburg
Rostock
Kaliningrad (RUSSIA)
Kaunas
Vilnius
Bremen
Szczecin
Gdańsk
Minsk
Mogilev
Bryansk
Hanover
Berlin
Bydgoszcz
Białystok
BELARUS
Gomel
GERMANY
Poznań
POLAND
Neman
Pripet
Dortmund
Leipzig
Warsaw
Brest
Dnieper
Cologne
Dresden
Łódź
Bug
Chernobyl
Bonn
Wrocław
Lublin
UKRAINE
Kiev
Frankfurt
Kraków
Zhitomir
CZECH REP.
Prague

ATLANTIC OCEAN

Baltic Sea

Gulf of Bothnia

Norrland

Svealand

Sveges / Sweden

Norway

Glåma

Torne

Muonio

Lule

Ume

Kemi

Tana

East from Greenwich

Scale 1:10 000 000   1cm on the map = 100 km on the ground

0   100km   200km   300km   400km   500km   600km

Height of the land (metres)

over 4000	
2000–4000	
1000–2000	
400–1000	
200–400	
0–200	
below sea level	

sea level

- ■ Over 5 000 000 inhabitants
- ● 1 000 000 – 5 000 000 inhabitants
- ● Under 1 000 000 inhabitants
- <u>Helsinki</u> Capital cities underlined
- —— Country boundaries
- ☐ Ice cap

COPYRIGHT PHILIP'S

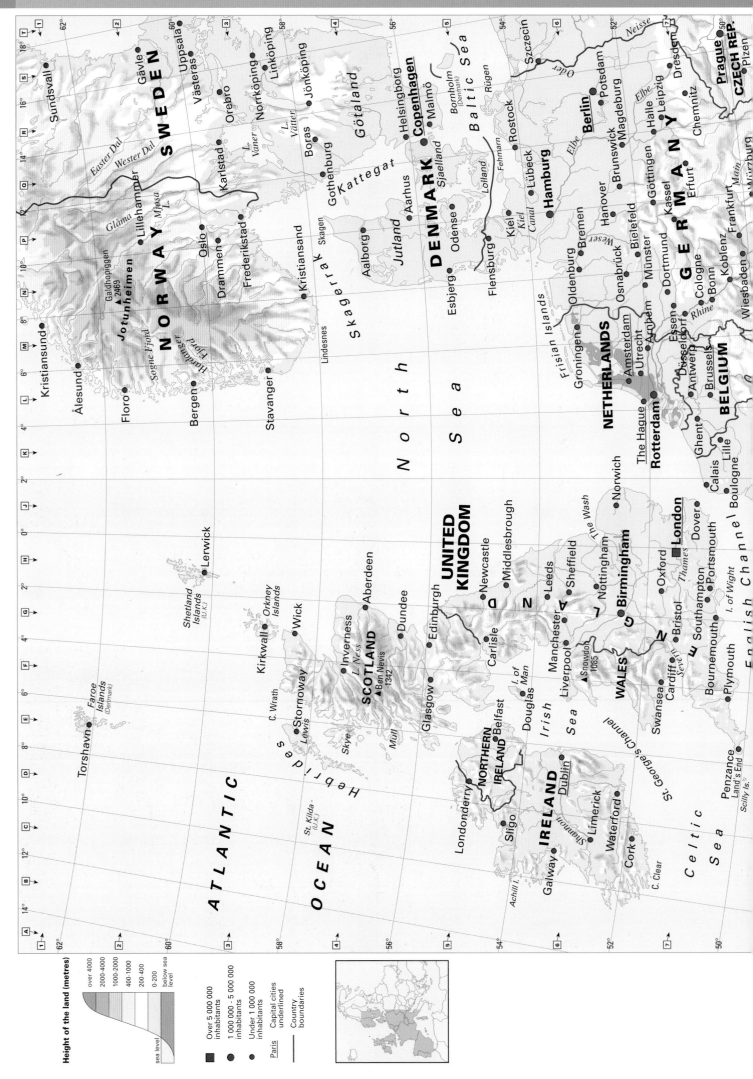

Height of the land (metres)

over 4000
2000-4000
1000-2000
400-1000
200-400
0-200
below sea level

sea level

● Over 5 000 000 inhabitants

● 1 000 000 - 5 000 000 inhabitants

● Under 1 000 000 inhabitants

Paris Capital cities underlined

—— Country boundaries

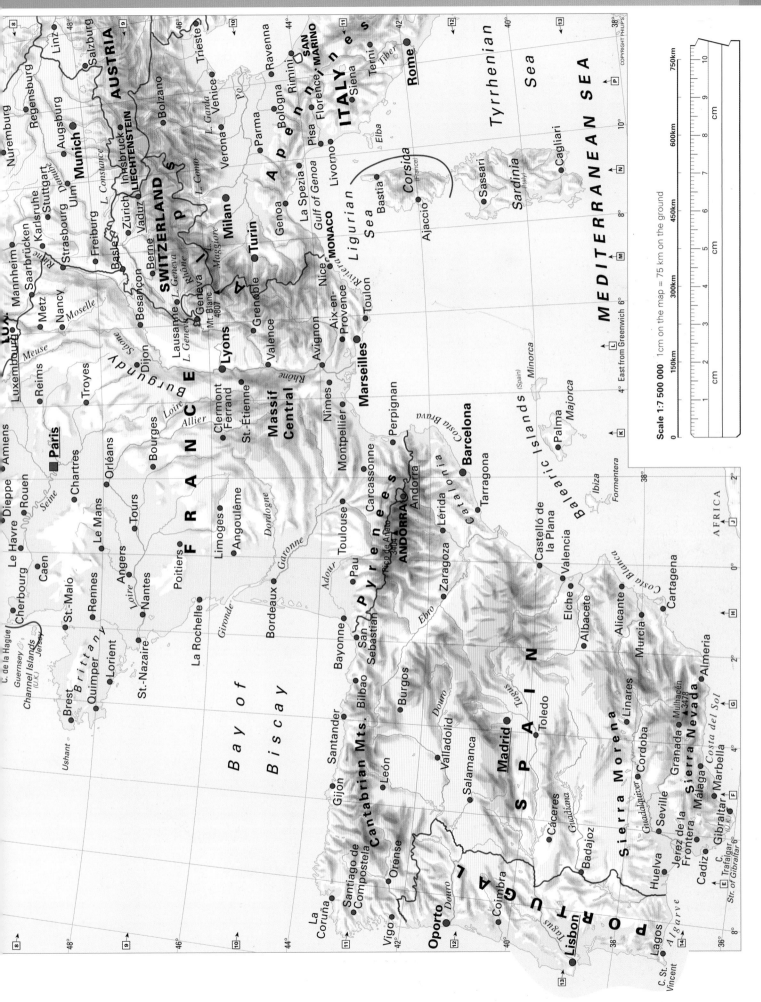

Scale 1:7 500 000 1cm on the map = 75 km on the ground

0	150km	300km	450km	600km	750km

cm 1 2 3 4 5 6 7 8 9 10

MEDITERRANEAN SEA

Tyrrhenian Sea

ITALY

Rome

SAN MARINO

Corsica (France)

Sardinia (Italy)

Cagliari

Sassari

Bastia

Ajaccio

Ligurian Sea

Genoa

La Spezia

Gulf of Genoa

Livorno

Pisa

Florence

Siena

Terni

Tiber

Elba

Ravenna

Rimini

Bologna

Parma

Po

Venice

Verona

L. Garda

Bolzano

Trieste

Milan

Turin

MONACO

Nice

Aix-en-Provence

Riviera

Toulon

Marseilles

Avignon

Nîmes

Montpellier

Perpignan

Grenoble

Valence

Mt. Blanc 4807

Geneva

L. Geneva

Lausanne

L. Maggiore

L. Como

L. Constance

Innsbruck

LIECHTENSTEIN

Vaduz

SWITZERLAND

Berne

Zürich

Basle

Besançon

Dijon

Rhône

Saône

Burgundy

Lyons

St-Étienne

Clermont Ferrand

Allier

Loire

Bourges

Massif Central

FRANCE

AUSTRIA

Salzburg

Linz

Regensburg

Nuremburg

Augsburg

Munich

Ulm

Danube

Stuttgart

Karlsruhe

Freiburg

Strasbourg

Saarbrücken

Mannheim

Metz

Nancy

Moselle

Meuse

LUX.

Luxembourg

Reims

Troyes

Paris

Seine

Amiens

Dieppe

Rouen

Le Havre

Cherbourg

C. de la Hague

Caen

St-Malo

Channel Islands (U.K.)

Guernsey

Jersey

Brittany

Brest

Quimper

Lorient

Ushant

Rennes

Le Mans

Angers

Nantes

St.-Nazaire

Loire

Tours

Chartres

Orléans

Poitiers

Angoulême

Limoges

Dordogne

La Rochelle

Bordeaux

Gironde

Garonne

Bay of Biscay

Adour

Bayonne

Pau

Pyrenees

Toulouse

Carcassonne

Andorra

ANDORRA

Pico de Aneto 3404

Catalonia

Lérida

Zaragoza

Ebro

Barcelona

Tarragona

Costa Brava

Balearic Islands (Spain)

Minorca

Majorca

Palma

Ibiza

Formentera

Castelló de la Plana

Valencia

Costa Blanca

Elche

Alicante

Albacete

Murcia

Cartagena

Almeria

AFRICA

Sierra Nevada

Mulhacén 3478

Granada

Costa del Sol

Málaga

Marbella

Gibraltar (U.K.)

C. Trafalgar

Str. of Gibraltar

Cádiz

Jerez de la Frontera

Guadalquivir

Córdoba

Linares

Sierra Morena

Seville

Huelva

Badajoz

Guadiana

Cáceres

SPAIN

Madrid

Toledo

Tagus

Salamanca

Valladolid

Douro

León

Burgos

Santander

Gijón

Cantabrian Mts.

Bilbao

San Sebastián

La Coruña

Santiago de Compostela

Orense

Vigo

Oporto

Douro

PORTUGAL

Coimbra

Tagus

Lisbon

Algarve

Lagos

C. St. Vincent

APENNINES

East from Greenwich

Height of the land (metres)

- over 4000
- 2000-4000
- 1000-2000
- 400-1000
- 200-400
- 0-200
- sea level
- below sea level

■ Over 5 000 000 inhabitants

● 1 000 000 - 5 000 000 inhabitants

• Under 1 000 000 inhabitants

<u>Sofia</u> Capital cities underlined

— Country boundaries

∴ Historical site

Seasonal lake

Scale 1:10 000 000 1cm on the map = 100 km on the ground

0   250km   500km   750km   1000km

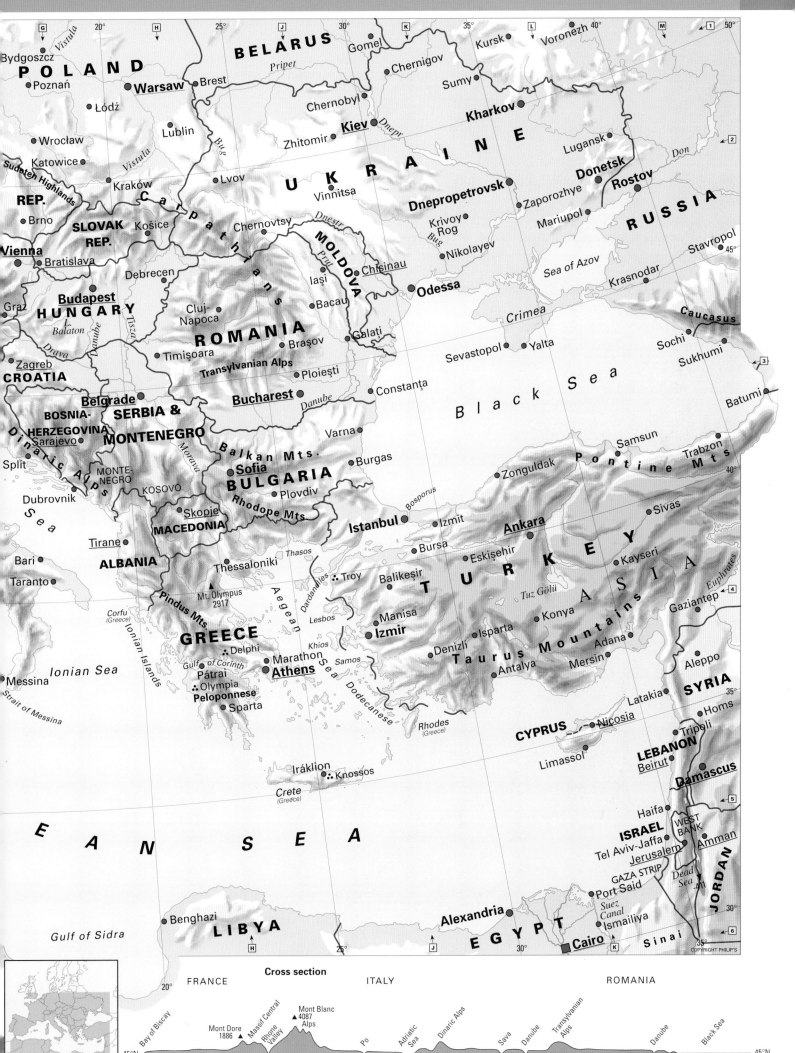

POLAND
Bydgoszcz
Poznań
Warsaw
Brest
Łódź
Wrocław
Katowice
Sudeten Highlands
Kraków
REP.
Brno
SLOVAK REP.
Košice
Vienna
Bratislava
Debrecen
Budapest
HUNGARY
Graz
L. Balaton
Zagreb
CROATIA
Belgrade
BOSNIA-HERZEGOVINA
Sarajevo
MONTENEGRO
MONTE-NEGRO
Split
Dinaric Alps
Dubrovnik
Sea
Bari
Taranto
Messina
Strait of Messina
Ionian Sea
Ionian Islands
Corfu (Greece)
Pindus Mts.
GREECE
Delphi
Gulf of Corinth
Pátrai
Olympia
Peloponnese
Sparta
Marathon
Athens
Iráklion
Knossos
Crete (Greece)

BELARUS
Gomel
Pripet
Vistula
Lublin
Bug
Vistula
Carpathians
Chernovtsy
MOLDOVA
Iaşi
Prut
Chişinău
Bacau
Cluj-Napoca
ROMANIA
Timişoara
Braşov
Transylvanian Alps
Ploieşti
Bucharest
Danube
SERBIA &
Morava
Balkan Mts.
Sofia
BULGARIA
Plovdiv
Rhodope Mts.
KOSOVO
Skopje
MACEDONIA
Tirane
ALBANIA
Thessaloniki
Thasos
Mt. Olympus 2917
Aegean
Dardanelles
Troy
Lesbos
Khios
Samos
Sea
Dodecanese
Rhodes (Greece)

Kursk
Voronezh
Chernigov
Sumy
Chernobyl
Kiev
Dnepr
Kharkov
Zhitomir
UKRAINE
Lugansk
Don
Vinnitsa
Lvov
Dnepropetrovsk
Donetsk
Rostov
Krivoy Rog
Zaporozhye
Bug
Nikolayev
Mariupol
RUSSIA
Odessa
Sea of Azov
Stavropol
Crimea
Krasnodar
Galaţi
Sevastopol
Yalta
Sochi
Sukhumi
Constanţa
Caucasus
Black Sea
Batumi
Varna
Burgas
Zonguldak
Pontine Mts.
Samsun
Trabzon
Bosporus
Istanbul
Izmit
Ankara
Sivas
Bursa
TURKEY
ASIA
Eskişehir
Balikeşir
Kayseri
Manisa
Konya
Euphrates
Izmir
Isparta
Gaziantep
Denizli
Taurus Mountains
Adana
Aleppo
Antalya
Mersin
Tuz Gölü

SYRIA
Latakia
Homs
CYPRUS
Nicosia
Tripoli
Limassol
LEBANON
Beirut
Damascus
Haifa
WEST BANK
ISRAEL
Amman
Tel Aviv-Jaffa
Jerusalem
GAZA STRIP
Dead Sea
Port Said
JORDAN
Suez Canal
Ismailiya
Sinai
Benghazi
LIBYA
Alexandria
EGYPT
Cairo
Gulf of Sidra

E A N   S E A

COPYRIGHT PHILIP'S

Cross section
FRANCE
ITALY
ROMANIA
Bay of Biscay
Mont Dore 1886
Massif Central
Rhone Valley
Mont Blanc 4087 Alps
Po
Adriatic Sea
Dinaric Alps
Sava
Danube
Transylvanian Alps
Danube
Black Sea
45°N
45°N

D North Sea 60° Bergen C 1 70° 10° 2 B 20° 3 80° 30° 4 40° 5 50° 6 60° 7

Franz Josef Land

A R C T I

N O R W A Y

DENMARK
Copenhagen

Bremen GERMANY
Hamburg
Elbe
Berlin

Oslo

S W E D E N

Narvik

L. Inari

North Cape

Barents Sea

Novaya Zemlya

Kara Sea

Bely I.

Gulf of Bothnia

FINLAND

Murmansk
Kola Peninsula

Kolguyev I.

Vaigach I.

Stockholm

Helsinki

Belomorsk
White Sea

Arctic Circle

Pechora

Gulf of Ob

Gothenburg

Malmö
Baltic Sea

Petrozavodsk

L. Onega

Mezen

Arkhangelsk

N. Dvina

Ukhta

Vorkuta

Novy Port

Igarka

Szczecin
Gdansk
Kaliningrad (Russia)
LITHUANIA
Vilnius
Riga
LATVIA
Tallinn
ESTONIA

St. Petersburg
Novgorod
Cherepovets
L. Ladoga

Kotlas

Narodnaya 1894

Ust Shchugor

Telpos Iz 1617

W e s t

Oder
POLAND
Lódz
Warsaw
Kraków
Vistula

Bialystok
Brest
Minsk
BELARUS

Tver

Vologda

Rybinsk
Yaroslavl

MOSCOW

Serov

Ob

S i b e r i a n

Zhitomir
Lvov
Dniestr
MOLDOVA
Chisinau

Mogilev
Gomel
Smolensk
Tula

Oka

Nizhniy
Novgorod

Kirov

Berezniki

Izhevsk

Perm

Narodnaya

Surgut

P l a i n

UKRAINE
Kiev
Krivoy Rog
Dnepr
Dnepropetrovsk
Zaporozhye

Orel
Kursk
Ryazan
Voronezh
Penza
Simbirsk

Volga

Kazan

Kama

Ufa

Yaman Tau 1640

Nizhniy Tagil
Yekaterinburg

Tyumen

Irtysh

Odessa
Donetsk
Rostov
Don

Saratov

Samara

Chelyabinsk

Omsk

Tomsk

Crimea
Sevastopol
Black Sea
Krasnodar
Sochi

Volgograd

Volga

Ural
Oral

Orenburg

Orsk

Magnitogorsk
Tobol

Ishim

Novosibirsk

Kemerovo
Novokuznetsk

Elbrus 5633
CAUCASUS

Astrakhan

Atyrau

Aqtobe

K A Z A K H S T A N

Pavlodar
Irtysh
Barnaul

Belukha 4506

GEORGIA
Tbilisi
Erzurum
L. Van
Yerevan
ARMENIA
AZERBAIJAN
Baku
Gyandzha

Grozny

C a s p i a n   S e a

Astana

Karaganda

Ust Kamenogorsk

Semey

A

Tabriz
L. Urmia

Aktau
Ust Urt Plateau

Aral Sea

Aralsk

Dzhezkazgan

Balkhash
L. Balkhash

Tarbagatai Ra.

Krasnovodsk
Kara Kum

Syr Darya

Kzyl Orda

SINKIANG
Dzungaria

Demavend 5604
Tehran
IRAN
Esfahan

TURKMENISTAN
Ashkhabad
Chardzhou
Samarkand
Bukhara
Kyzyl Kum

UZBEKISTAN
Tashkent

Chimkent

Bishkek
KYRGYZSTAN
Alma Ata
Ürümqi

Mashhad

Amu Darya

TAJIKISTAN
Dushanbe

Andizhan
Pk. Pobedy 7439

CHINA
Turfan

Yazd
30°
6
60°
7
East from Greenwich 80°
8
9
90°

Communism Pk. 7495

Height of the land (metres)

| over 6000 |
| 4000-6000 |
| 2000-4000 |
| 1000-2000 |
| 400-1000 |
| 200-400 |
| 0-200 |
| below sea level |

sea level

■ Over 5 000 000 inhabitants

● 1 000 000 - 5 000 000 inhabitants

• Under 1 000 000 inhabitants

Kiev Capital cities underlined

—— Country boundaries

OCEAN

Komsomolets I.

October Revolution I.

Bolshevik I.

Severnaya
Zemlya

Boris Vilkitski Str.
C. Chelyuskin

Laptev
Sea

New Siberian Is.

East Siberian Sea

Wrangel I.

Anadyr Range

Gulf of Anadyr

60°

Nizhne Kolymsk

Anadyr

Kolyma
Range

Anadyr

Bering
Sea

D

Taimyr

Peninsula

Nordvik

Tiksi

Olenek

Lyakhov Is.

Dimitri Laptev Str.

Yana

Verkhoyansk

Cherskiy Range

Oymyakon

Kolyma

Gizhiga

Shelekhov
Gulf

Kamchatka
Peninsula

Khatanga

Kotuy

Verkhoyansk

Okhotsk

Magadan

Sredinnyy
Range

Petropavlovsk-
Kamchatskiy

Norilsk

Lena

Range

Arctic Circle

Sea of
Okhotsk

50°

Central

Yakutsk

Aldan

Siberian

Olekminsk

Shantar Is.

Sakhalin

Lower Tunguska

Plateau

Aldan

Aldan

Aleksandrovsk

Stony Tunguska

SIA

Stanovoy Range

Kuril Islands

E

Angara

Vitim

Sikhote

Yuzhno-
Sakhalinsk

b

e

Yablonovyy Range

Amur

Alin

Kansk

Ust-Ilimsk

Bratsk

Lena

Amur

Komsomolsk

Khabarovsk

Asahikawa

Krasnoyarsk

Nizhneudinsk

Angara

Blagoveshchensk

L. Khanka

Hokkaido

Sapporo

Abakan

L. Baikal

Chita

Hegang

Sungari

Sendai

Hakodate

40°

Ubsa Nur

Angarsk

Munku Sardyk
3491

Irkutsk

Ulan Ude

Hailar

Qiqihar

CHINA

Harbin

Vladivostok

Akita

Manzhouli

Sungari

Hakodate

Khangai Mts

Ulan Bator

Manchuria

Sea of

Honshu

JAPAN

Sendai

a

i

MONGOLIA

Gobi

Kirin

Sungari
Res.

Japan

Tokyo

n

G o b i

INNER
MONGOLIA

Changchun

Fushun

Shenyang

Anshan

NORTH KOREA

Pyongyang

Seoul

SOUTH KOREA

Kobe
Osaka

Yokohama

Nagoya

COPYRIGHT PHILIP'S

70° 80° 90° 100° 110° 120° 130°

Scale 1:20 000 000   1cm on the map = 200 km on the ground

0   500km   1000km   1500km   2000km   2500km

1   2   3   4   5   6   7   8   9   10

cm   cm   cm

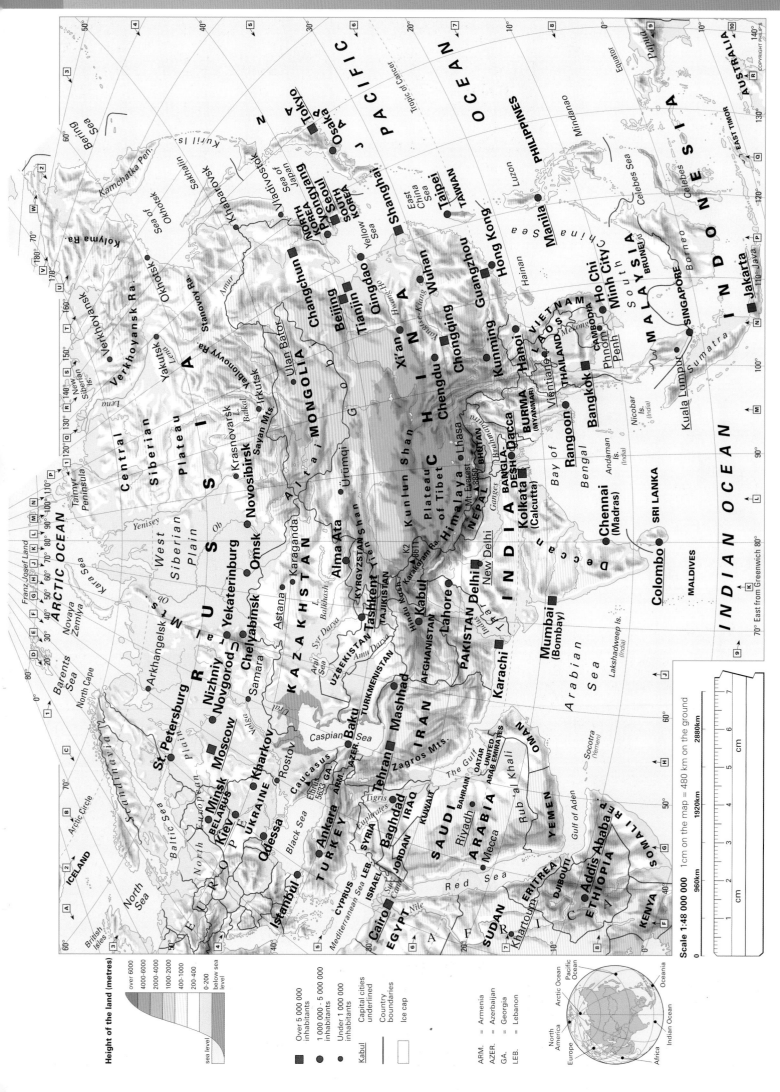

Scale 1:48 000 000 1cm on the map = 480 km on the ground

Height of the land (metres)

over 6000
4000-6000
2000-4000
1000-2000
400-1000
200-400
0-200
below sea level

sea level

Over 5 000 000 inhabitants
1 000 000 - 5 000 000 inhabitants
Under 1 000 000 inhabitants

Kabul Capital cities underlined

Country boundaries

Ice cap

ARM. = Armenia
AZER. = Azerbaijan
GA. = Georgia
LEB. = Lebanon

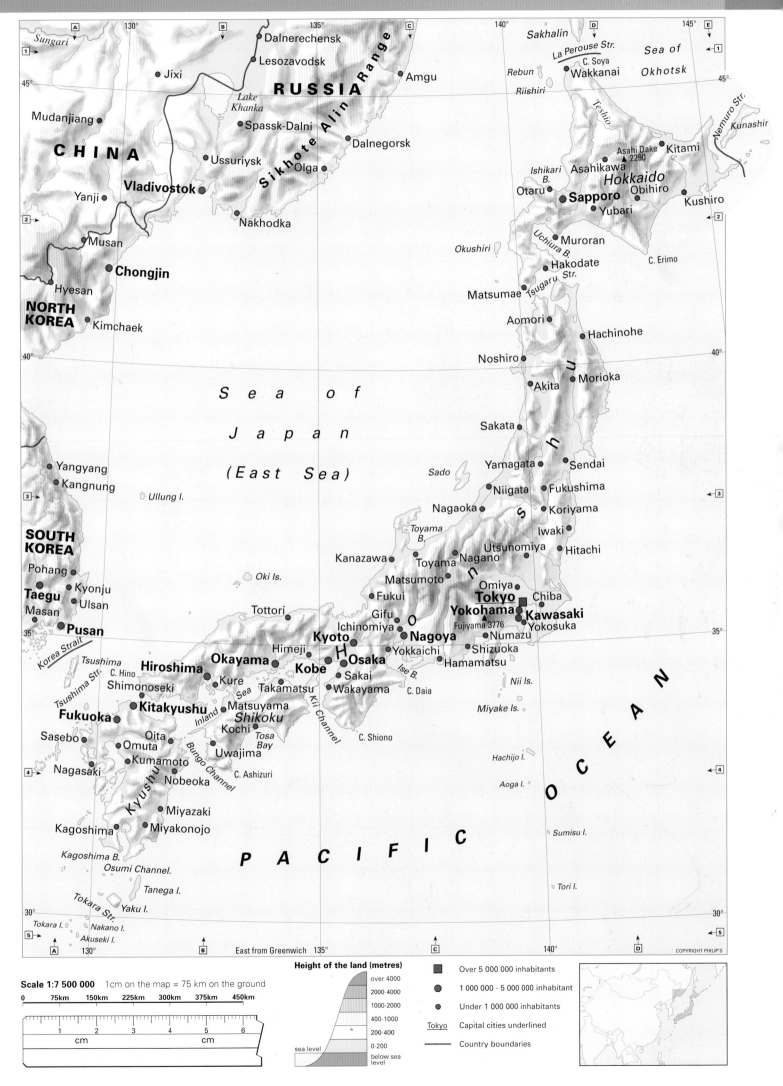

Scale 1:7 500 000   1cm on the map = 75 km on the ground

0   75km   150km   225km   300km   375km   450km

Height of the land (metres)

over 4000
2000–4000
1000–2000
400–1000
200–400
0–200
sea level
below sea level

◼ Over 5 000 000 inhabitants

● 1 000 000 – 5 000 000 inhabitant

● Under 1 000 000 inhabitants

Tokyo   Capital cities underlined

──   Country boundaries

COPYRIGHT PHILIP'S

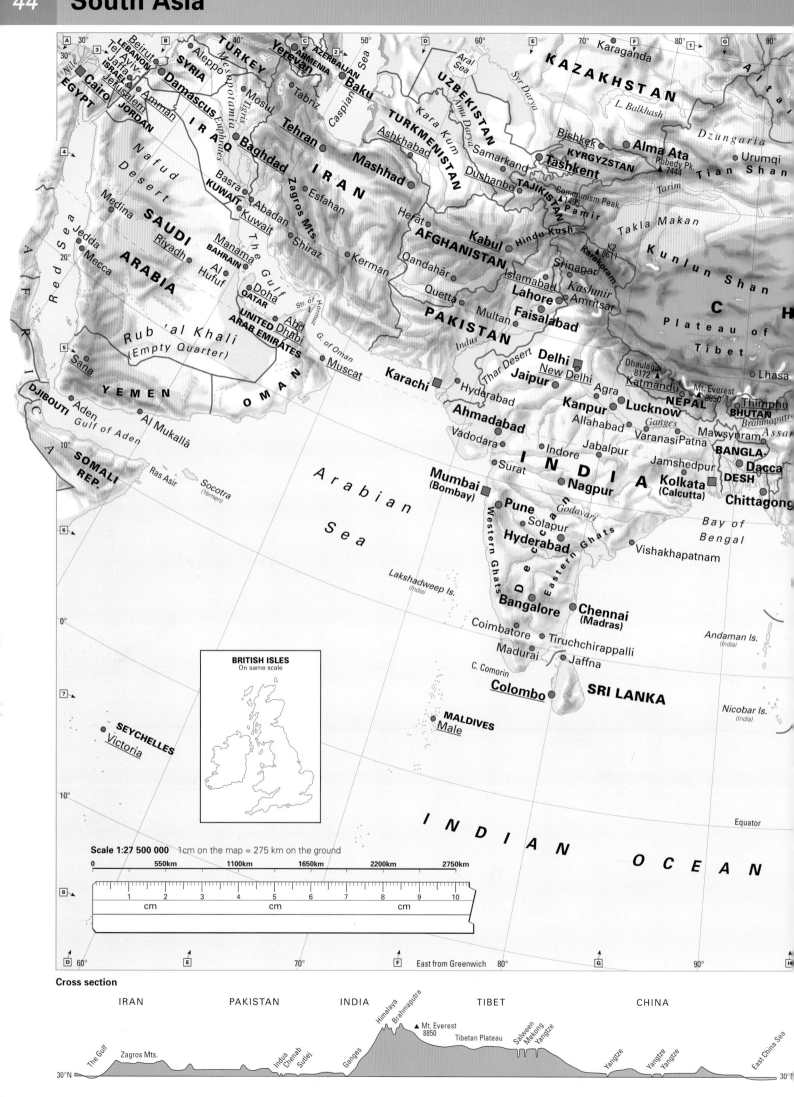

Scale 1:27 500 000 1cm on the map = 275 km on the ground

0	550km	1100km	1650km	2200km	2750km

BRITISH ISLES
On same scale

Cross section

IRAN   PAKISTAN   INDIA   TIBET   CHINA

H 100° J 110° 1 K 120° L 130° M 140° N O 150° P 160° Q

Qiqihar
Manchuria
Harbin
RUSSIA
Vladivostok
Sapporo
Hokkaido
Sea of Japan
30°

MONGOLIA
Plateau of Mongolia
Ulan Bator
Gobi
Inner Mongolia
Great Khingan
Changchun
Shenyang Fushun
Anshan
NORTH KOREA
Pyongyang
Sendai
Honshu
JAPAN
Tokyo
Yokohama

Nan Shan
Beijing
Tianjin
GREAT WALL
Dalian
SOUTH KOREA
Seoul
Pusan
Yellow Sea
Kyoto Kobe Nagoya
Osaka
Hiroshima
Shikoku
Kitakyushu
Kyushu

Lanzhou
Taiyuan
Hwang-Ho
Grand Canal
Qingdao

C H I N A
Xi'an
Nanjing
Shanghai
East China Sea
PACIFIC OCEAN
Bonin Is. (Japan)
Tropic of Cancer
20°

Chengdu
Wuhan
Hangzhou
Yangtze-Kiang
Three Gorges Dam

Chongqing
Changsha
Nanchang
Fuzhou
Taipei
TAIWAN
Kaohsiung
Ryukyu Is.

NORTHERN MARIANAS (U.S.A.)

Guiyang

Kunming
Guangzhou
Nanning
Macau Hong Kong
Guam (U.S.A.)
10°

FEDERATED STATES OF MICRONESIA

BURMA
Mandalay
(MYANMAR)
Hanoi
Haiphong
LAOS
Gulf of Tonkin
Hainan
Luzon
Quezon City
Manila
PHILIPPINES

Irrawaddy
Salween
Chiengmai
Vientiane
VIETNAM
Mekong
Da Nang
South China Sea
PALAU
6

Rangoon
Moulmein
THAILAND
Bangkok
CAMBODIA
Phnom Penh
Ho Chi Minh City
Gulf of Thailand
Palawan
Sulu Sea
Cebu
Mindanao
Davao

Zamboanga
Sulu Arch.
0°

Malay Peninsula
Songkhla
Kota Kinabalu
Sabah
BRUNEI
Bandar Seri Begawan
Sarawak
Celebes Sea
Manado
Halmahera
Papua

George Town
MALAYSIA
Kuching
Borneo
East
Moluccas
Seram
Aru Is.
7

Medan
Str. of Malacca
Kuala Lumpur
Putrajaya
SINGAPORE
Pontianak
I n d i e s
Celebes
Buru
Banda Sea
Tanimbar
Arafura Sea
10°

Sumatra
Padang
Bangka
INDONESIA
Banjarmasin
Ujung Pandang
Flores Sea
Dili EAST TIMOR
Timor
Darwin
8

Palembang
Jakarta
Bandung
Semarang Surabaya
Java
Sunda Islands
Lombok
Bali Sumbawa
Flores
Sumba
Timor Sea
AUSTRALIA
130° M
COPYRIGHT PHILIP'S

100° J 110° K 120° L

Height of the land (metres)
over 6000
4000-6000
2000-4000
1000-2000
400-1000
200-400
0-200
sea level
below sea level

Over 5 000 000 inhabitants
1 000 000 - 5 000 000 inhabitants
Under 1 000 000 inhabitants
Beijing Capital cities underlined
Country boundaries
Seasonal lakes
Ice

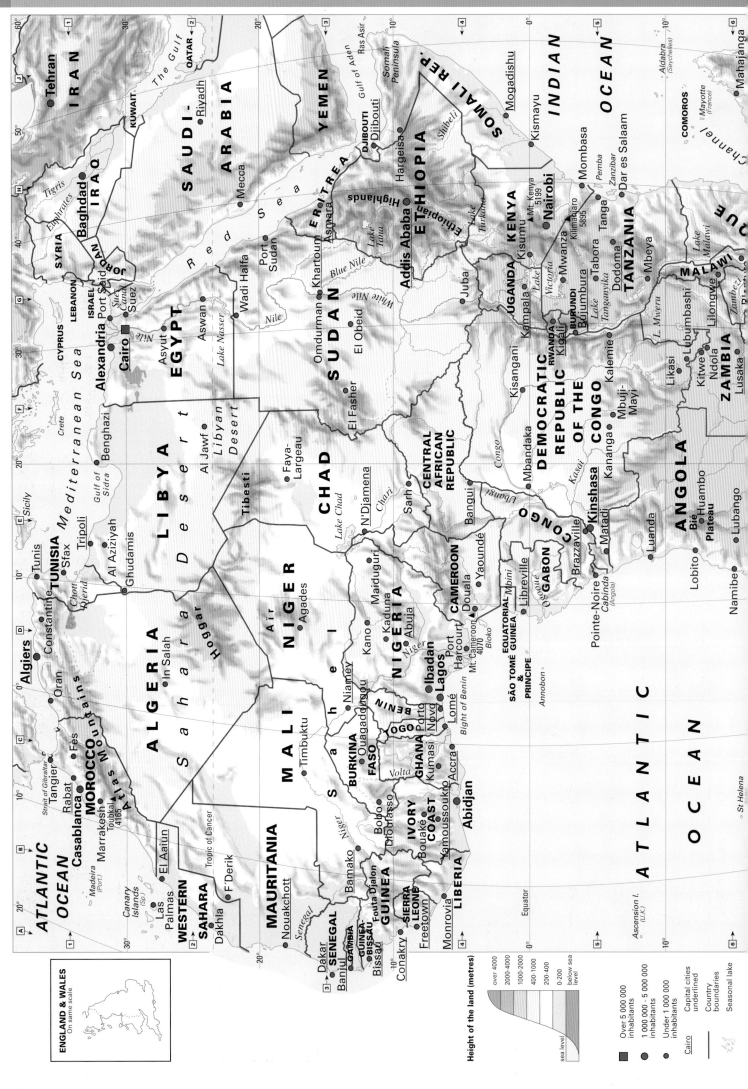

ENGLAND & WALES
On same scale

Height of the land (metres)
over 4000
2000-4000
1000-2000
400-1000
200-400
0-200
below sea level

sea level

■ Over 5 000 000 inhabitants
● 1 000 000 - 5 000 000 inhabitants
● Under 1 000 000 inhabitants

Cairo Capital cities underlined
——— Country boundaries
Seasonal lake

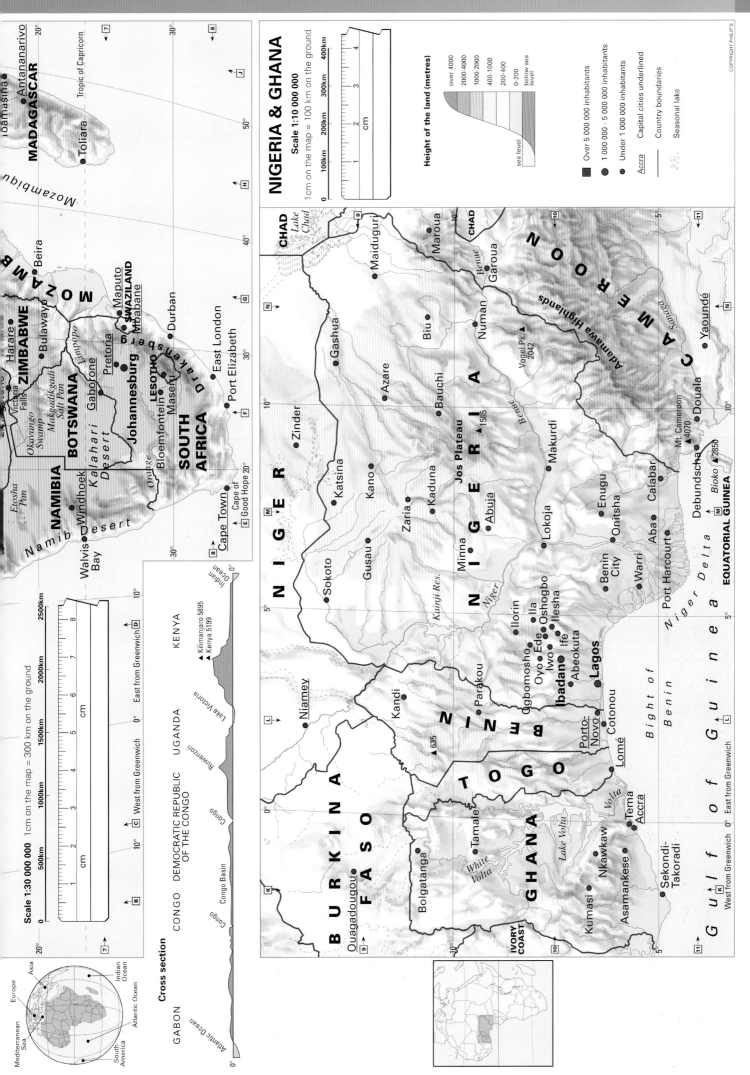

NIGERIA & GHANA

Scale 1:10 000 000

1cm on the map = 100 km on the ground

Height of the land (metres)

over 4000
2000-4000
1000-2000
400-1000
200-400
0-200
below sea level

Over 5 000 000 inhabitants

1 000 000 - 5 000 000 inhabitants

Under 1 000 000 inhabitants

Accra Capital cities underlined

Country boundaries

Seasonal lake

COPYRIGHT PHILIP'S

Scale 1:30 000 000

1cm on the map = 300 km on the ground

Cross section

GABON CONGO DEMOCRATIC REPUBLIC OF THE CONGO UGANDA KENYA

Congo Basin

▲ Kilimanjaro 5895
▲ Kenya 5199

Lake Victoria

Ruwenzori

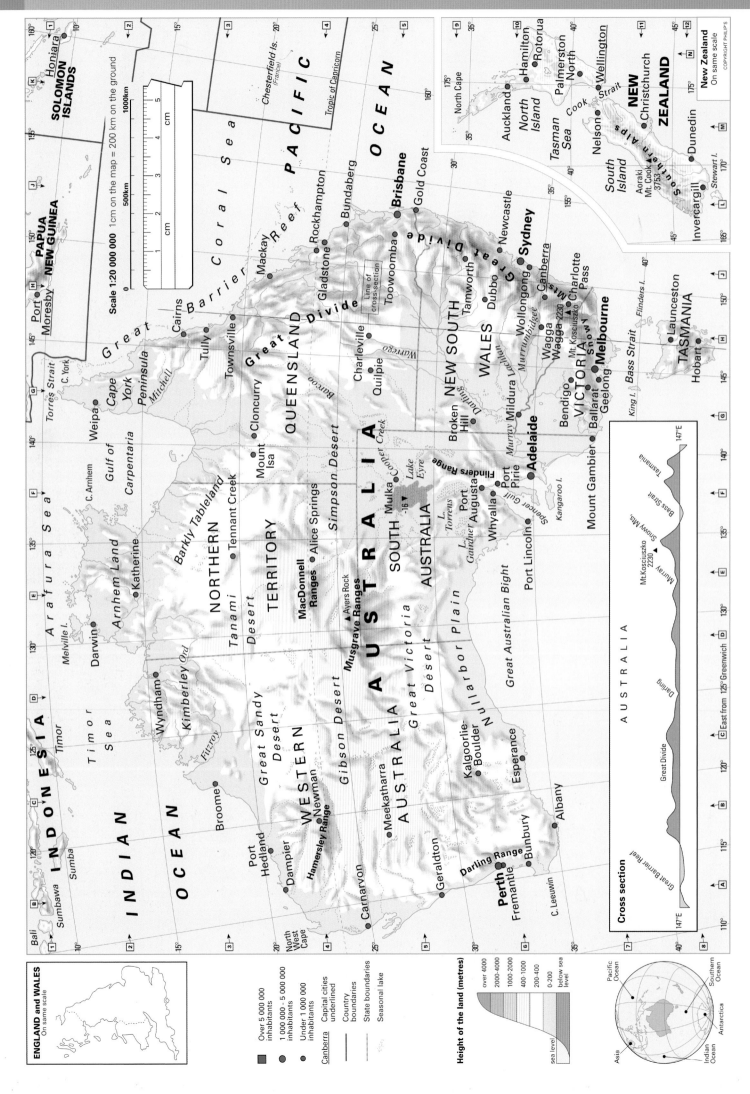

New Zealand
On same scale

NEW
ZEALAND

North Cape
Auckland
North Island
Hamilton
Rotorua
Tasman Sea
Cook Strait
Nelson
Palmerston North
Wellington
Christchurch
Southern Alps
South Island
Aoraki Mt. Cook 3753
Dunedin
Stewart I.
Invercargill

SOLOMON ISLANDS
Honiara

PACIFIC OCEAN

PAPUA NEW GUINEA
Port Moresby

Chesterfield Is. (France)

Coral Sea

Tropic of Capricorn

Scale 1:20 000 000
1cm on the map = 200 km on the ground

Cairns
Great Barrier Reef
Townsville
Tully
Mackay
Rockhampton
Gladstone
Bundaberg
Brisbane
Gold Coast
Toowoomba
Great Divide
Newcastle
Sydney
Wollongong
Canberra
Line of cross-section

QUEENSLAND
Great Dividing
Charleville
Quilpie
Warrego
Barcoo

NEW SOUTH WALES
Tamworth
Dubbo
Murrumbidgee
Wagga Wagga
Mt. Kosciuszko 2230
Charlotte Pass
Snowy
Melbourne

Cape York
C. York
Torres Strait
Cape York Peninsula
Mitchell
Weipa

Gulf of Carpentaria
C. Arnhem

Arafura Sea

Arnhem Land
Darwin
Melville I.
Timor Sea

INDONESIA
Bali
Sumbawa
Sumba
Timor

INDIAN OCEAN

Kimberley
Ord
Wyndham
Fitzroy

NORTHERN TERRITORY
Barkly Tableland
Tennant Creek
Tanami Desert
Katherine

Cloncurry
Mount Isa
Simpson Desert

Alice Springs
MacDonnell Ranges
Ayers Rock
Musgrave Ranges

SOUTH AUSTRALIA
Cooper Creek
Lake Eyre
Mulka -16
Flinders Range
L. Torrens
L. Gairdner

Broken Hill
Mildura
Murray
Darling
Bendigo
Ballarat
VICTORIA
Geelong
Mount Gambier

Adelaide
Port Pirie
Port Augusta
Whyalla
Spencer Gulf
Port Lincoln
Kangaroo I.

King I.
Bass Strait
Flinders I.
TASMANIA
Launceston
Hobart

WESTERN AUSTRALIA
Great Sandy Desert
Gibson Desert
Great Victoria Desert
Nullarbor Plain
Great Australian Bight

Broome
Port Hedland
Dampier
Hamersley Range
Newman
Meekatharra
Kalgoorlie-Boulder
Esperance
Geraldton
Carnarvon
North West Cape
Darling Range
Perth
Fremantle
Bunbury
Albany
C. Leeuwin

A U S T R A L I A

Cross section
Great Barrier Reef
Great Divide
Darling
Murray
Mt.Kosciuszko 2230
Snowy Mts.
Bass Strait
Tasmania
Pacific Ocean
sea level
147°E
East from 125° Greenwich
147°E

ENGLAND AND WALES
On same scale

Over 5 000 000 inhabitants
1 000 000 - 5 000 000 inhabitants
Under 1 000 000 inhabitants
Canberra Capital cities underlined
Country boundaries
State boundaries
Seasonal lake

Height of the land (metres)
over 4000
2000-4000
1000-2000
400-1000
200-400
0-200
below sea level
sea level

Pacific Ocean
Asia
Indian Ocean
Antarctica
Southern Ocean

COPYRIGHT PHILIPS

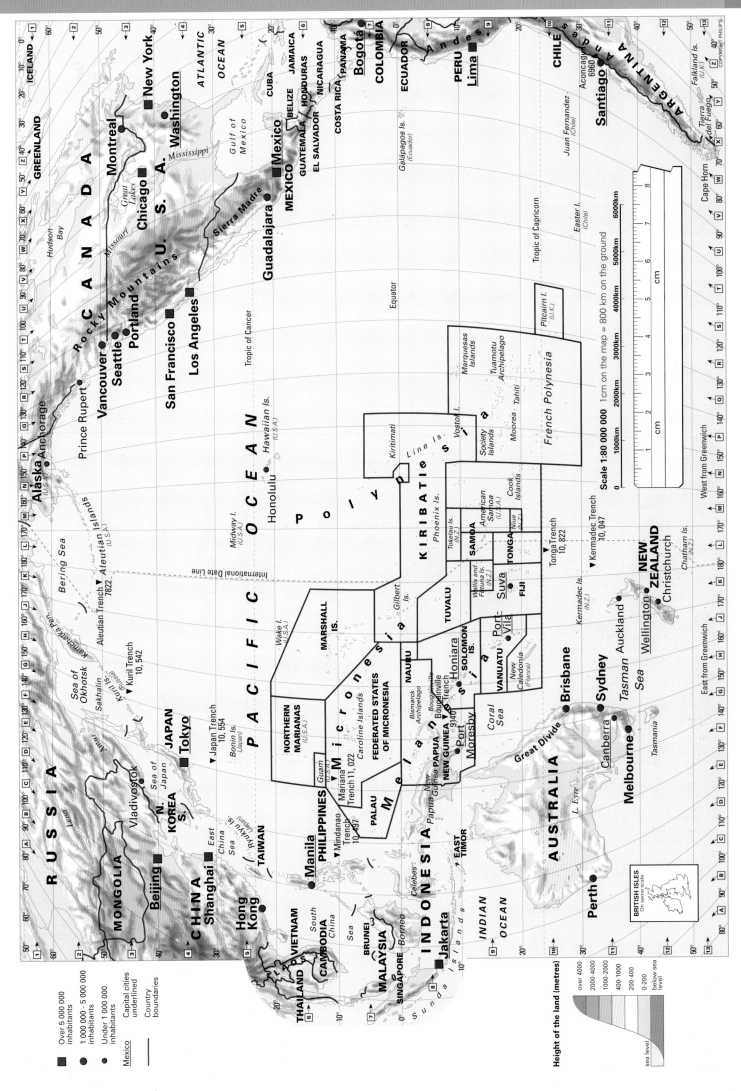

Height of the land (metres)

over 4000
2000-4000
1000-2000
400-1000
200-400
0-200
below sea level

Over 5 000 000 inhabitants

1 000 000 - 5 000 000 inhabitants

Under 1 000 000 inhabitants

Mexico Capital cities underlined

Country boundaries

BRITISH ISLES
On same scale

Scale 1:80 000 000 1cm on the map = 800 km on the ground

0 1000km 2000km 3000km 4000km 5000km 6000km

West from Greenwich

East from Greenwich

COPYRIGHT PHILIP'S

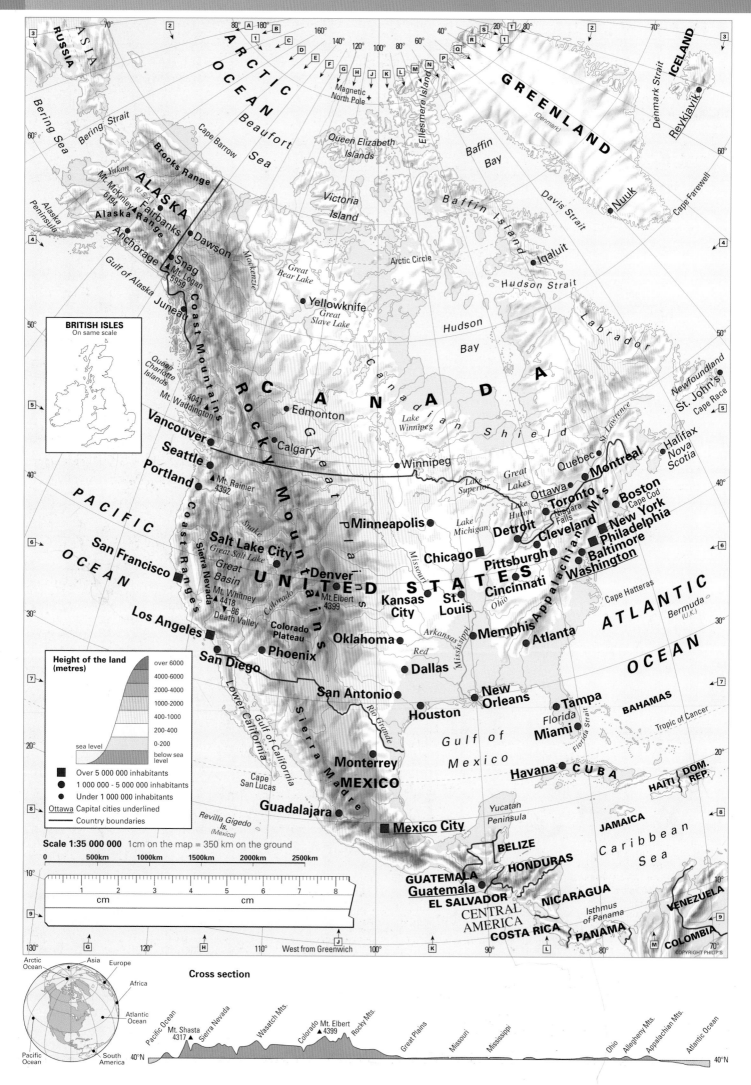

North America

ASIA
RUSSIA
ARCTIC OCEAN
Bering Sea
Bering Strait
Beaufort Sea
Cape Barrow
Queen Elizabeth Islands
Ellesmere Island
Magnetic North Pole
GREENLAND (Denmark)
ICELAND
Reykjavik
Denmark Strait
Alaska Peninsula
Yukon
Mt. McKinley (U.S.) 6194
ALASKA
Fairbanks
Brooks Range
Alaska Range
Anchorage
Dawson
Snag
Mt. Logan 5959
Gulf of Alaska
Juneau
Coast Mountains
Mackenzie
Great Bear Lake
Victoria Island
Baffin Bay
Baffin Island
Cape Farewell
Nuuk
Queen Charlotte Islands
Mt. Waddington 4041
Rocky Mountains
CANADA
Yellowknife
Great Slave Lake
Arctic Circle
Hudson Strait
Davis Strait
Iqaluit
Labrador
Hudson Bay
Vancouver
Seattle
Portland
Mt. Rainier 4392
Edmonton
Calgary
Winnipeg
Lake Winnipeg
Great Plains
Canadian Shield
Lake Superior
Great Lakes
St. Lawrence
Newfoundland
St. John's
Cape Race
Halifax
Nova Scotia
PACIFIC OCEAN
San Francisco
Salt Lake City
Great Salt Lake
Sierra Nevada
Snake
Great Basin
UNITED STATES
Denver
Mt. Elbert 4399
Minneapolis
Lake Michigan
Lake Huron
Chicago
Detroit
Quebec
Ottawa
Toronto
Montreal
Niagara Falls
Cleveland
Pittsburgh
Boston
Cape Cod
New York
Philadelphia
Baltimore
Washington
Appalachian Mts.
Coast Ranges
Mt. Whitney 4418
Death Valley -86
Colorado
Colorado Plateau
Kansas City
St. Louis
Cincinnati
Missouri
Ohio
ATLANTIC OCEAN
Cape Hatteras
Bermuda (U.K.)
Los Angeles
San Diego
Phoenix
Oklahoma
Dallas
Red
Arkansas
Mississippi
Memphis
Atlanta
Lower California
San Antonio
Houston
New Orleans
Rio Grande
Gulf of Mexico
Tampa
Florida
Miami
Florida Strait
BAHAMAS
Tropic of Cancer
Sierra Madre
Monterrey
MEXICO
Cape San Lucas
Gulf of California
Havana
CUBA
HAITI
DOM. REP.
Guadalajara
Revilla Gigedo Is. (Mexico)
Mexico City
Yucatan Peninsula
JAMAICA
Caribbean Sea
BELIZE
GUATEMALA
Guatemala
EL SALVADOR
HONDURAS
NICARAGUA
CENTRAL AMERICA
COSTA RICA
Isthmus of Panama
PANAMA
VENEZUELA
COLOMBIA

BRITISH ISLES
On same scale

Height of the land (metres)
over 6000
4000-6000
2000-4000
1000-2000
400-1000
200-400
0-200
sea level
below sea level

■ Over 5 000 000 inhabitants
● 1 000 000 - 5 000 000 inhabitants
• Under 1 000 000 inhabitants
Ottawa Capital cities underlined
— Country boundaries

Scale 1:35 000 000 1cm on the map = 350 km on the ground

0 500km 1000km 1500km 2000km 2500km

cm cm

West from Greenwich

COPYRIGHT PHILIP'S

Cross section

Arctic Ocean
Asia
Europe
Africa
Atlantic Ocean
Pacific Ocean
South America

Pacific Ocean
Mt. Shasta 4317
Sierra Nevada
Wasatch Mts.
Colorado
Mt. Elbert 4399
Rocky Mts.
Great Plains
Missouri
Mississippi
Ohio
Allegheny Mts.
Appalachian Mts.
Atlantic Ocean
40°N
40°N

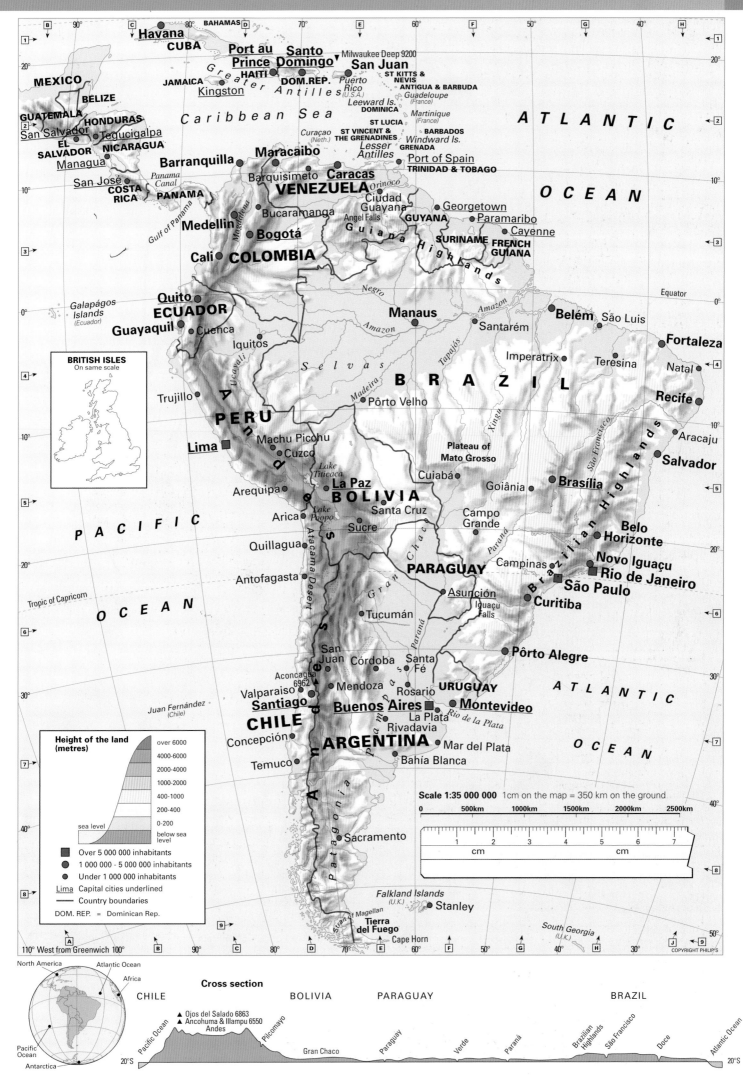

Havana
CUBA
BAHAMAS
Milwaukee Deep 9200
Port au
Prince
Santo
Domingo
San Juan
St KITTS &
NEVIS
MEXICO
HAITI
JAMAICA
Greater
Antilles
DOM.REP.
Puerto
Rico
(U.S.A.)
ANTIGUA & BARBUDA
Guadeloupe
(France)
BELIZE
Kingston
Leeward Is.
DOMINICA
GUATEMALA
HONDURAS
Caribbean Sea
Martinique
(France)
ST LUCIA
GUATEMALA
San Salvador
Tegucigalpa
Curaçao
(Neth.)
ST VINCENT &
THE GRENADINES
BARBADOS
EL
SALVADOR
NICARAGUA
Lesser
Antilles
Windward Is.
GRENADA
Managua
Barranquilla
Maracaibo
Port of Spain
TRINIDAD & TOBAGO
San José
COSTA
RICA
PANAMA
Panama
Canal
Barquisimeto
Caracas
ATLANTIC
Gulf of Panama
Bucaramanga
VENEZUELA
Orinoco
OCEAN
Medellin
Ciudad
Guayana
Georgetown
Paramaribo
Magdalena
Angel Falls
GUYANA
Cayenne
Bogotá
Guiana
Highlands
SURINAME
FRENCH
GUIANA
Cali
COLOMBIA
Negro
Equator
Galápagos
Islands
(Ecuador)
Quito
ECUADOR
Manaus
Amazon
Belém
São Luis
Guayaquil
Cuenca
Santarém
Fortaleza
Iquitos
Amazon
Ucayali
Selvas
Tapajós
Natal
BRITISH ISLES
On same scale
B R A Z I L
Imperatrix
Teresina
Trujillo
Madeira
Pôrto Velho
Recife
PERU
Andes
Xingu
São Francisco
Aracaju
Lima
Machu Picchu
Cuzco
Salvador
Plateau of
Mato Grosso
Brazilian Highlands
Lake
Titicaca
Cuiabá
Brasília
Arequipa
La Paz
BOLIVIA
Goiânia
Belo
Horizonte
Arica
Lake
Poopó
Sucre
Santa Cruz
Campo
Grande
Campinas
Novo Iguaçu
Rio de Janeiro
Quillagua
Atacama Desert
PARAGUAY
Paraná
São Paulo
Antofagasta
Gran Chaco
Asunción
Iguaçu
Falls
Curitiba
Tropic of Capricorn
Paraná
PACIFIC
Tucumán
Pôrto Alegre
OCEAN
San
Juan
Córdoba
Santa
Fé
Aconcagua
6962
Mendoza
Rosario
URUGUAY
ATLANTIC
Juan Fernández
(Chile)
Valparaiso
Santiago
Buenos Aires
Montevideo
La Plata
Río de la Plata
CHILE
ARGENTINA
Rivadavia
Mar del Plata
Concepción
Bahía Blanca
OCEAN
Temuco
Andes
Pampas
Patagonia
Sacramento

Height of the land
(metres)
over 6000
4000–6000
2000–4000
1000–2000
400–1000
200–400
sea level
0–200
below sea
level
◼ Over 5 000 000 inhabitants
● 1 000 000 – 5 000 000 inhabitants
• Under 1 000 000 inhabitants
Lima Capital cities underlined
— Country boundaries
DOM. REP. = Dominican Rep.

Scale 1:35 000 000   1cm on the map = 350 km on the ground
0   500km   1000km   1500km   2000km   2500km

Falkland Islands
(U.K.)
Stanley
Strait of Magellan
Tierra
del Fuego
South Georgia
(U.K.)
Cape Horn
110° West from Greenwich 100°
COPYRIGHT PHILIP'S

North America
Atlantic Ocean
Africa
Cross section
CHILE
BOLIVIA
PARAGUAY
BRAZIL
Pacific
Ocean
▲ Ojos del Salado 6863
▲ Ancohuma & Illampu 6550
Andes
Pacific
Ocean
Antarctica
Pilcomayo
Gran Chaco
Paraguay
Paraguay
Verde
Paraná
Brazilian
Highlands
São Francisco
Doce
Atlantic Ocean
20°S

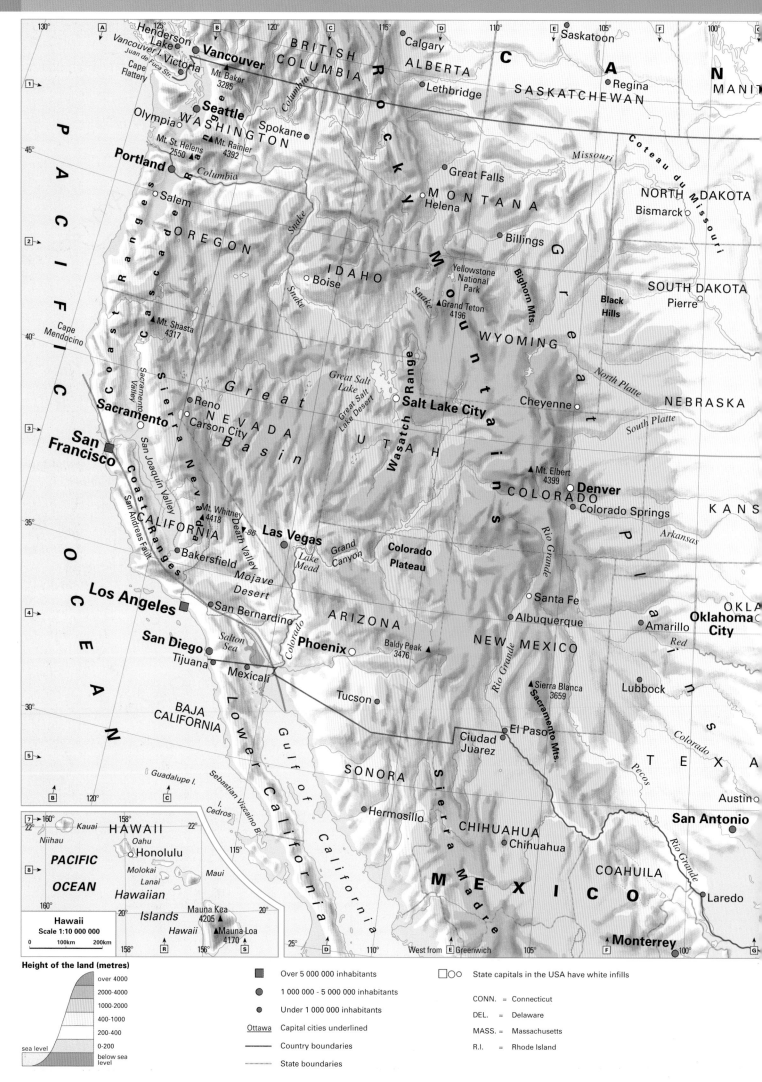

Height of the land (metres)

	over 4000
	2000-4000
	1000-2000
	400-1000
	200-400
sea level	0-200
	below sea level

■ Over 5 000 000 inhabitants

● 1 000 000 - 5 000 000 inhabitants

• Under 1 000 000 inhabitants

Ottawa Capital cities underlined

Country boundaries

State boundaries

□○○ State capitals in the USA have white infills

CONN. = Connecticut

DEL. = Delaware

MASS. = Massachusetts

R.I. = Rhode Island

95° H 90° J 85° K 80° L 75° M 70° N 65°

Lake Winnipeg

A D A

OBA

Winnipeg

MANITOBA

QUEBEC

NEW BRUNSWICK

1

O N T A R I O

St. Lawrence

MAINE

45°

Fargo

Duluth

Thunder Bay

Lake Superior

Sault Ste.Marie

Sudbury

Ottawa

Quebec

Montreal

Ottawa

VERMONT

Montpelier

Mt. Washington 1917

NEW HAMPSHIRE

Augusta

Portland

2

Mississippi

MINNESOTA

Minneapolis

St. Paul

WISCONSIN

G r e a t   L a k e s

Georgian Bay

MICHIGAN

Lake Huron

Toronto

Lake Ontario

Rochester

NEW YORK

Albany

Hamilton

Buffalo

Concord

New England

MASS.

Boston

C. Cod

R.I. Providence

Hartford

CONN.

Madison

Milwaukee

Lake Michigan

Lansing

Detroit

Lake Erie

Cleveland

PENNSYLVANIA

Long I.

40°

Chicago

Toledo

Pittsburgh

Harrisburg

NEW

Trenton

New York

Philadelphia

JERSEY

IOWA

M i d w e s t

OHIO

Columbus

Dayton

Baltimore

Dover

Des Moines

ILLINOIS

INDIANA

MARYLAND

Annapolis

DEL.

Delaware Bay

3

Omaha

Springfield

Indianapolis

Cincinatti

Ohio

WEST VIRGINIA

Washington D.C.

Potomac

Chesapeake Bay

Lincoln

Missouri

Mississippi

Charleston

VIRGINIA

Richmond

Topeka

Kansas City

St. Louis

Louisville

Frankfort

Norfolk

35°

Jefferson City

MISSOURI

Lake of the Ozarks

Ohio

KENTUCKY

Cumberland

Raleigh

Pamlico Sd.

C. Hatteras

AS

Ozark Plateau

TENNESSEE

Cumberland Plateau

Nashville

Tennessee

A p p a l a c h i a n   M t s.

Blue Ridge

NORTH CAROLINA

Charlotte

HOMA

Arkansas

ARKANSAS

Memphis

SOUTH CAROLINA

Columbia

C. Fear

4

Little Rock

Birmingham

Atlanta

Savannah

Mississippi

MISSISSIPPI

ALABAMA

GEORGIA

Columbus

Savannah

Dallas

Sabine

Jackson

Montgomery

Tombigbee

Alabama

Chattahoochee

30°

Fort Worth

Trinity

LOUISIANA

Brazos

S

Baton Rouge

Jacksonville

Tallahassee

L. Pontchartrain

New Orleans

Cape San Blas

5

Houston

Delta of the Mississippi

Orlando

C. Canaveral

Indian River

A T L A N T I C   O C E A N

Tampa

Tampa B.

FLORIDA

L. Okeechobee

Grand Bahama I.

Great Abaco

G u l f   o f   M e x i c o

Everglades

Miami

BAHAMAS

Nassau

Eleuthera I.

25°

Laguna Madre

Florida Keys

Florida Str.

Andros I.

Long I.

Cat I.

6

95° H 90° J 85° K 80° L 75° M

COPYRIGHT PHILIP'S

Scale 1:12 000 000 1cm on the map = 120 km on the ground

0 200km 400km 600km 800km 1000km 1200km

1 2 3 4 5 6 7 8 9 10

cm cm cm

Tijuana
Mexicali
Bataques
115°
A
Phoenix
110°
B
Tucson
El Paso
105°
C
Ciudad Juárez
100°
D
Dallas
95°
E
Birmingham
90°
F
G

UNITED STATES

Rio Grande
Pecos
Texas
Austin
Houston
San Antonio
New Orleans
Mississippi
Alabama
Mississippi Delta

30°

Hermosillo
Sonora
Yaqui
▲ 2896
Chihuahua
Conchos
Nuevo Laredo
Corpus Christi

Ciudad Obregón
Sierra Madre
▲ 3150

25°

Los Mochis
Torreón
Reynosa
Matamoros
Monterrey

Gulf of Mexico

La Paz
Culiacan
Durango
▲ 4054

Lower California
Gulf of California
Colorado

C. San Lucas

3

Mazatlán
Rio Grande de Santiago
MEXICO
Madre
3353 ▲
San Luis Potosí
Aguascalientes
Tampico
Tropic of Cancer

Las Tres Marias
León

20°

C. Corrientes
Guadalajara
Querétaro
Mérida
Cancún
Yucatan Str.

Revilla Gigedo Is.
Popocatepetl
5610
Gulf of Campeche
Campeche

Mexico
5452 ▲
Pico de Orizaba
Yucatan

4

Cuernavaca
Puebla

Balsas

Villahermosa
Belmopan
Belize City
Gulf of Honduras

Acapulco
Oaxaca
Isthmus of Tehuantepec
Chiapa
Tuxtla Gutiérrez
BELIZE

15°

Gulf of Tehuantepec
4217 ▲
Puerto Barrios
San Pedro Sula
GUATEMALA
HONDURAS

P A C I F I C

5

Guatemala
Tegucigal
San Salvador
EL SALVADOR
NICARA

Managua
L. Nicaragu

10°

O C E A N

6

ENGLAND and WALES
On same scale

5°

7

110°
B
105°
C
100°
D
West from Greenwich
95°
F
90°
G

Height of the land (metres)

over 4000
2000-4000
1000-2000
400-1000
200-400
0-200
below sea level
sea level

◼ Over 5 000 000 inhabitants

● 1 000 000 - 5 000 000 inhabitants

• Under 1 000 000 inhabitants

<u>Mexico</u>   Capital cities underlined

——   Country boundaries

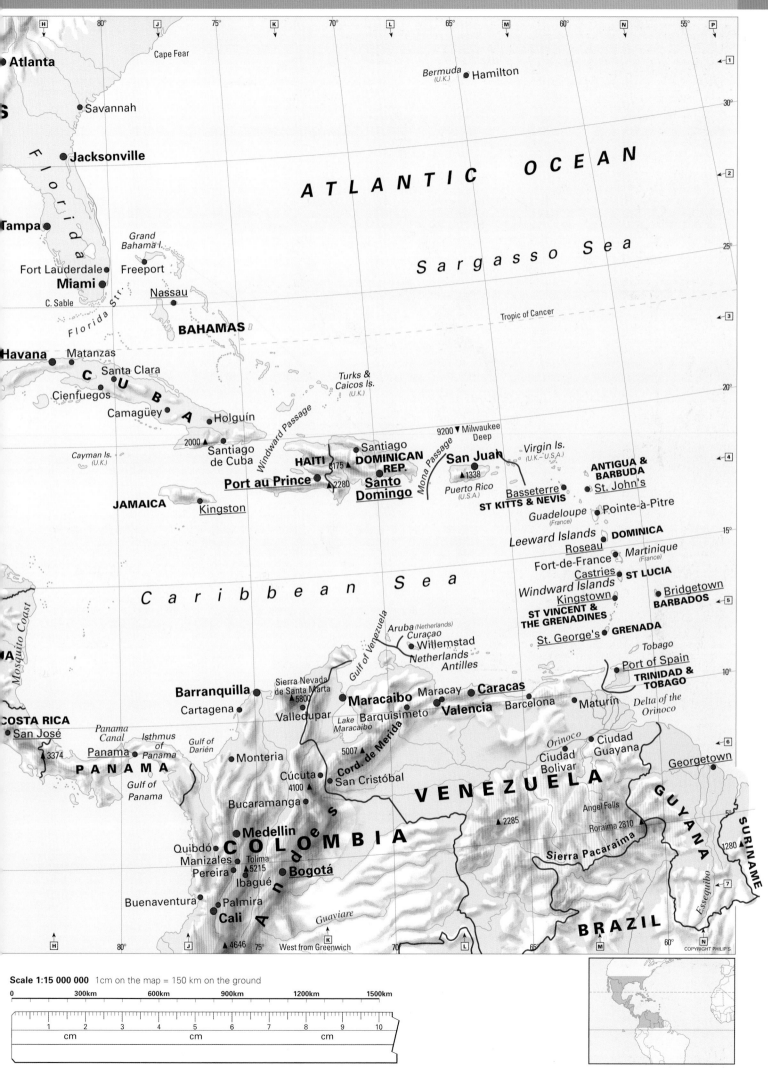

Scale 1:15 000 000 1cm on the map = 150 km on the ground

0   300km   600km   900km   1200km   1500km

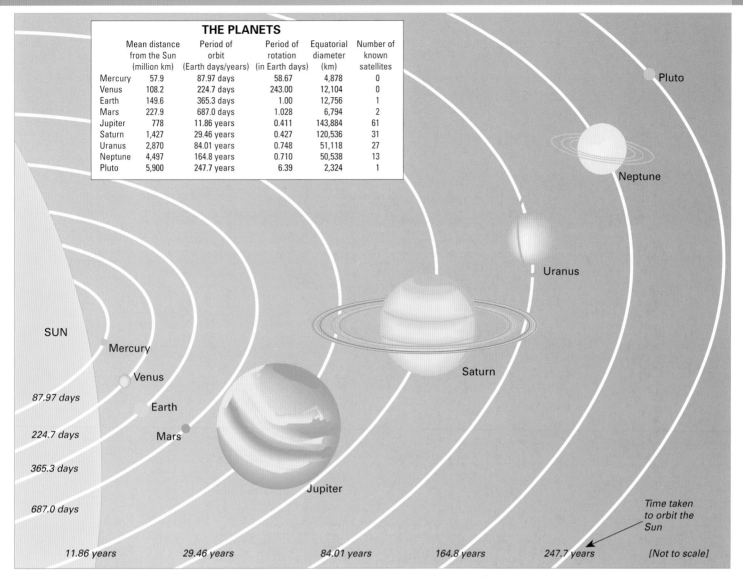

THE PLANETS				
	Mean distance from the Sun (million km)	Period of orbit (Earth days/years)	Period of rotation (in Earth days)	Equatorial diameter (km)	Number of known satellites
Mercury	57.9	87.97 days	58.67	4,878	0
Venus	108.2	224.7 days	243.00	12,104	0
Earth	149.6	365.3 days	1.00	12,756	1
Mars	227.9	687.0 days	1.028	6,794	2
Jupiter	778	11.86 years	0.411	143,884	61
Saturn	1,427	29.46 years	0.427	120,536	31
Uranus	2,870	84.01 years	0.748	51,118	27
Neptune	4,497	164.8 years	0.710	50,538	13
Pluto	5,900	247.7 years	6.39	2,324	1

THE SOLAR SYSTEM

The Universe is made up of many galaxies, or collections of stars. Our galaxy is called the Milky Way. It is made up of about 100,000 million stars. The Sun is one of these stars. Around it revolve nine planets, one of which is the Earth. The Sun, its planets and their satellites are known as the Solar System. The Sun is the only source of light and heat in the Solar System. The other planets are visible from the Earth because of the sunlight which they reflect. The planets orbit the Sun in the same direction – anti-clockwise when viewed from the northern hemisphere – and almost in the same plane. They also spin on their own axes. The planets remain in orbit because they are attracted by the Sun's pull of gravity.

THE MOON

Some of the planets have satellites that revolve around them. The Earth has just one satellite, called the Moon, which takes just over 27 days to rotate on its own axis as well as to revolve around the Earth. As a result, the Moon presents the same face to us, and we never see 'the dark side'. The diagrams on the left show how the Moon appears to have different shapes at different times of the month. These are known as the 'phases of the Moon'. The Earth is nearly always between the Sun's rays and the Moon and casts a shadow on to it. The apparent changes in the shape of the Moon are caused by its changing position in relation to both the Earth and the rays of the Sun.

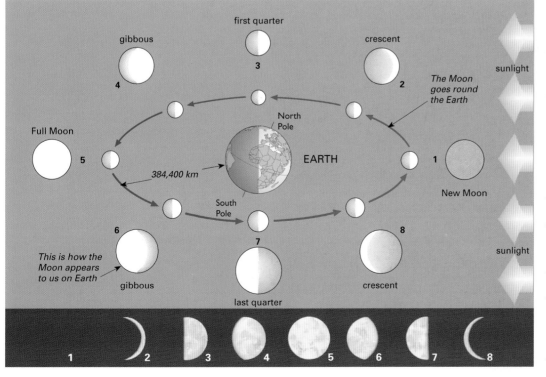

Continent	Area, '000 km	Coldest place, °C		Hottest place, °C		Wettest place (average annual rainfall, mm)		Driest place (average annual rainfall, mm)
Asia	44,500	Oymyakon, Russia -70°C	①	Tirat Zevi, Israel 54°C	⑧	Mawsynram, India 11,870	⑮	Aden, Yemen 46
Africa	30,302	Ifrane, Morocco -24°C	②	Al Aziziyah, Libya 58°C	⑨	Debundscha, Cameroon 10,290	⑯	Wadi Haifa, Sudan 2
North America	24,241	Snag, Yukon -63°C	③	Ifrane, Morocco -24°C	⑩	Henderson Lake, Canada 6,500	⑰	Bataques, Mexico 30
South America	17,793	Sarmiento, Argentina -33°C	④	Death Valley, California 57°C	⑪	Quibdó, Colombia 8,990	⑱	Quillagua, Chile 0.5
Antarctica	14,000	Vostok -89°C	⑤	Vanda Station 15°C	⑫			
Europe	9,957	Ust'Shchugor, Russia -55°C	⑥	Seville, Spain 50°C	⑬	Crkvice, Serbia & M. 4,650	⑲	Astrakhan, Russia 160
Oceania	8,557	Charlotte Pass, Australia -22°C	⑦	Cloncurry, Australia 53°C	⑭	Tully, Australia 4,550	⑳	Muika, Australia 100

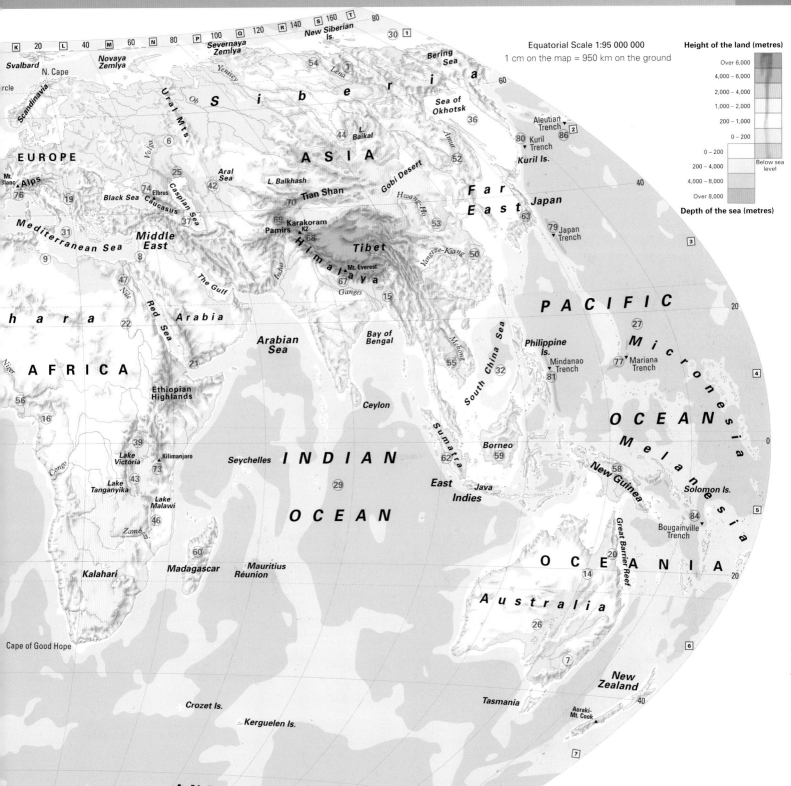

World - largest seas	'000 km²		World - largest lakes	'000 km²		World - longest rivers, km			World - largest islands	'000 km²		World - Highest peaks, m		World - deepest trenches, m	
Pacific Ocean 165,721		27	Caspian Sea 424		37	Nile 6,690		47	Greenland 2,176		57	Himalayas:Mt.Everest 8,850	67	Mariana Trench 11,022	77
Atlantic Ocean 81,660		29	Lake Superior 82		38	Amazon 6,280		48	New Guinea 777		58	Karakoram Ra:K2 8,611	68	Tonga Trench 10,822	78
Indian Ocean 73,442		28	Lake Victoria 69		39	Mississippi -Missouri 6,270		49	Borneo 725		59	Pamirs:Communism Pk. 7,495	69	Japan Trench 10,554	79
Arctic Ocean 14,351		30	Lake Huron 60		40	Yangtze-Kiang 4,990		50	Madagascar 590		60	Tian Shan: Pik Pobedy 7,439	70	Kuril Trench 10,542	80
Mediterranean Sea 2,966		31	Lake Michigan 58		41	Congo 4,670		51	Baffin Island 476		61	Andes:Aconcagua 6,962	71	Mindanao Trench 10,497	81
South China Sea 2,318		32	Aral Sea 36		42	Amur 4,410		52	Sumatra 474		62	Rocky Mts:Mt.McKinley 6,194	72	Kermadec Trench 10,047	82
Bering Sea 2,274		33	Lake Tanganyika 33		43	Hwang-Ho 4,350		43	Honshu 228		63	East Africa: Mt.Kilimanjaro 5,895	73	Milwaukee Deep 9,200	83
Caribbean Sea 1,942		34	Lake Baikal 31		44	Lena 4,260		54	Great Britain 217		64	Caucasus:Elbrus 5,633	74	Bougainville Trench 9,140	84
Gulf of Mexico 1,813		35	Great Bear Lake 31		45	Mekong 4,180		55	Victoria Island 212		65	Antarctica:Vinson Massif 5,140	75	South Sandwich Island Trench 8,428	85
Sea of Okhotsk 1,528		36	Lake Malawi 31		46	Niger 4,180		56	Ellesmere Island 197		66	Alps:Mt. Blanc 4,810	76	Aleutian Trench 7,822	86

Country	Population in thousands 2003 estimate	Area in thous' km²	Country	Population in thousands 2003 estimate	Area in thous' km²	Country	Population in thousands 2003 estimate	Area in thous' km²	Country	Population in thousands 2003 estimate	Area in thous' km²	Country	Population in thousands 2003 estimate	Area in thous' km²	Country	Population in thousands 2003 estimate	Area in thous' km²
China	1 286 975	9 597	Mexico	104 908	1 973	United Kingdom	60 095	245	Poland	38 623	313	Uzbekistan	25 982	447
India	1 049 700	3 288	Philippines	84 620	300	Italy	57 998	301	Sudan	38 114	2 506	Uganda	25 633	236
United States	290 343	9 629	Germany	82 398	357	Congo, Dem. Rep.	56 625	2 345	Tanzania	35 922	945	Iraq	24 683	437
Indonesia	234 893	1 919	Vietnam	81 625	330	Korea, South	48 289	98	Algeria	32 819	2 382	Venezuela	24 655	912
Brazil	182 033	8 512	Egypt	74 719	1 001	Ukraine	48 055	604	Canada	32 207	9 976	Saudi Arabia	25 294	1 961
Pakistan	150 695	804	Iran	68 279	1 648	South Africa	42 769	1 220	Morocco	31 689	447	Malaysia	23 093	330
Russia	144 526	17 075	Turkey	68 109	781	Burma (Myanmar)	42 511	679	Kenya	31 639	583	Taiwan	22 603	36
Bangladesh	138 448	144	Ethiopia	66 558	1 127	Colombia	41 662	1 139	Afghanistan	28 717	648	Korea, North	22 466	121
Nigeria	133 882	924	Thailand	64 265	514	Spain	40 217	505	Peru	28 410	1 285	Romania	22 272	238
Japan	127 214	378	France	60 181	547	Argentina	38 741	2 767	Nepal	26 470	141	Ghana	20 468	239

Equatorial Scale 1:95 000 000
1 cm on the map = 950 km on the ground

Country	Population in thousands 2003 estimate	Area in thous' km²	Country	Population in thousands 2003 estimate	Area in thous' km²	Country	Population in thousands 2003 estimate	Area in thous' km²	Country	Population in thousands 2003 estimate	Area in thous' km²	Country	Population in thousands 2003 estimate	Area in thous' km²
Sri Lanka	19 742	66	Chile	15 665	757	Angola	10 766	1 247	Tunisia	9 925	164	Bulgaria	7 538	111
Australia	19 732	7 687	Guatemala	13 909	109	Greece	10 666	132	Chad	9 253	1 284	Haiti	7 528	28
Yemen	19 350	528	Ecuador	13 710	284	Serbia and Mont.	10 656	102	Guinea	9 030	246	Hong Kong	7 394	1
Syria	17 586	185	Burkina Faso	13 228	274	Senegal	10 580	196	Sweden	8 878	450	Switzerland	7 319	41
Mozambique	17 479	802	Cambodia	13 125	181	Belarus	10 322	208	Dominican Republic	8 716	49	Benin	7 041	113
Madagascar	16 980	587	Zimbabwe	12 577	391	Zambia	10 307	753	Bolivia	8 586	1 099	Tajikistan	6 864	143
Ivory Coast	16 962	322	Malawi	11 651	118	Belgium	10 289	31	Austria	8 188	84	Honduras	6 670	112
Kazakhstan	16 764	2 717	Mali	11 626	1 240	Czech Republic	10 249	79	Somalia	8 025	638	El Salvador	6 470	21
Netherlands	16 151	42	Cuba	11 263	111	Portugal	10 102	92	Azerbaijan	7 831	87	Israel	6 117	21
Cameroon	15 746	475	Niger	11 059	1 267	Hungary	10 045	93	Rwanda	7 810	26	Burundi	6 096	28

COPYRIGHT PHILIP'S

CLIMATE REGIONS

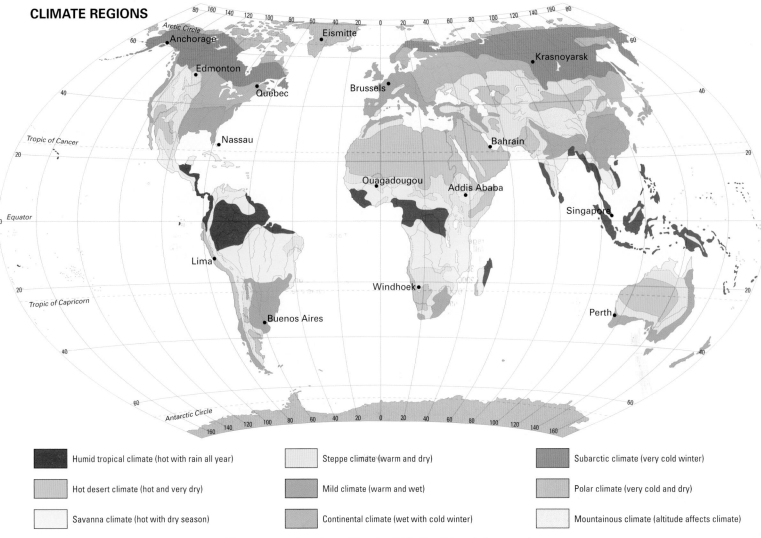

Humid tropical climate (hot with rain all year)	Steppe climate (warm and dry)	Subarctic climate (very cold winter)
Hot desert climate (hot and very dry)	Mild climate (warm and wet)	Polar climate (very cold and dry)
Savanna climate (hot with dry season)	Continental climate (wet with cold winter)	Mountainous climate (altitude affects climate)

The map shows how the world can be divided into 9 broad climate regions.

CLIMATE GRAPHS

The graphs below give examples of places within each climate region, showing how temperature and rainfall vary from month to month.

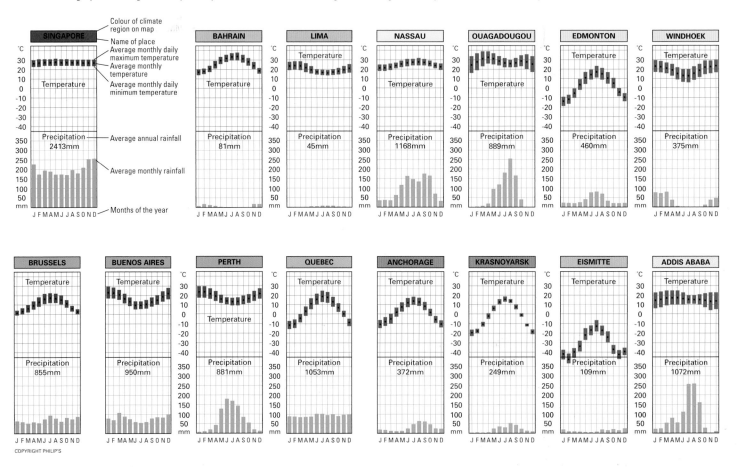

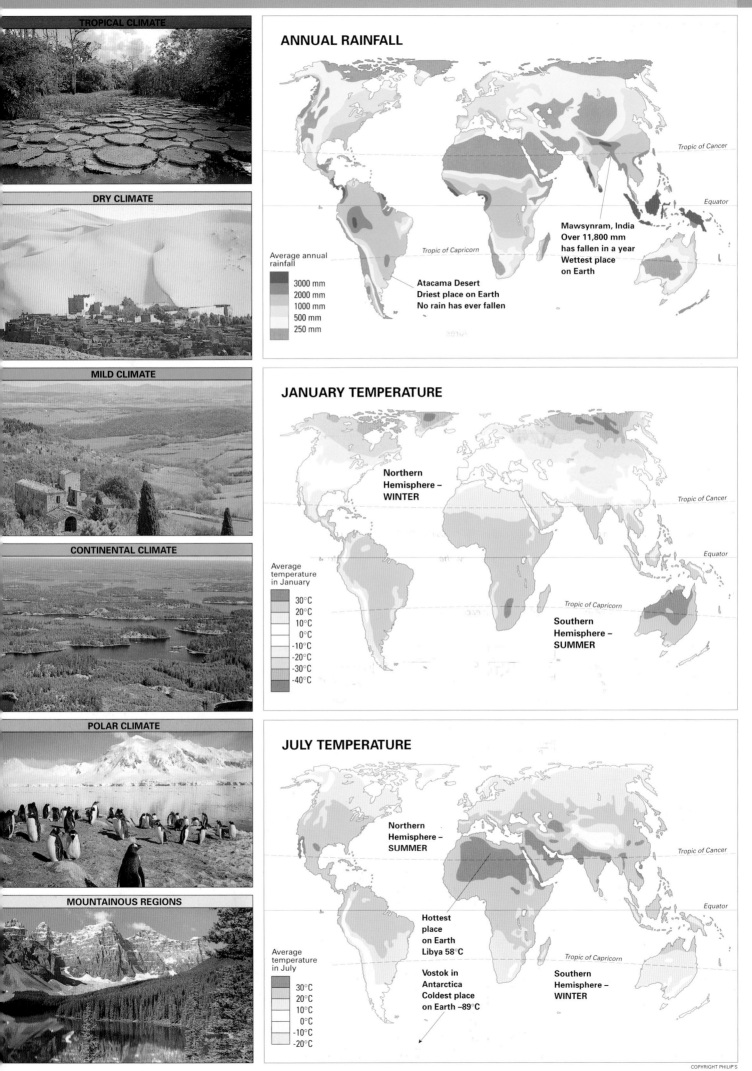

TROPICAL CLIMATE

DRY CLIMATE

MILD CLIMATE

CONTINENTAL CLIMATE

POLAR CLIMATE

MOUNTAINOUS REGIONS

ANNUAL RAINFALL

Tropic of Cancer

Equator

Tropic of Capricorn

Average annual
rainfall

- 3000 mm
- 2000 mm
- 1000 mm
- 500 mm
- 250 mm

**Atacama Desert
Driest place on Earth
No rain has ever fallen**

**Mawsynram, India
Over 11,800 mm
has fallen in a year
Wettest place
on Earth**

JANUARY TEMPERATURE

**Northern
Hemisphere –
WINTER**

Tropic of Cancer

Equator

Tropic of Capricorn

**Southern
Hemisphere –
SUMMER**

Average
temperature
in January

- 30°C
- 20°C
- 10°C
- 0°C
- -10°C
- -20°C
- -30°C
- -40°C

JULY TEMPERATURE

**Northern
Hemisphere –
SUMMER**

Tropic of Cancer

Equator

**Hottest
place
on Earth
Libya 58°C**

**Vostok in
Antarctica
Coldest place
on Earth –89°C**

Tropic of Capricorn

**Southern
Hemisphere –
WINTER**

Average
temperature
in July

- 30°C
- 20°C
- 10°C
- 0°C
- -10°C
- -20°C

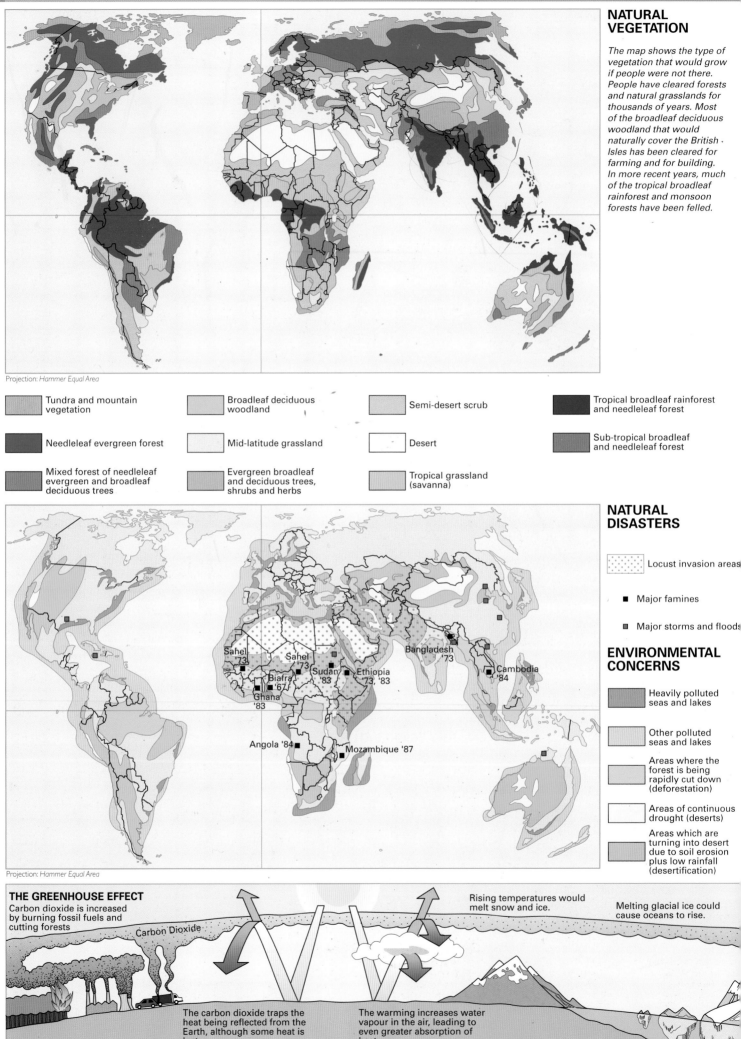

NATURAL VEGETATION

The map shows the type of vegetation that would grow if people were not there. People have cleared forests and natural grasslands for thousands of years. Most of the broadleaf deciduous woodland that would naturally cover the British Isles has been cleared for farming and for building. In more recent years, much of the tropical broadleaf rainforest and monsoon forests have been felled.

Projection: *Hammer Equal Area*

- Tundra and mountain vegetation
- Needleleaf evergreen forest
- Mixed forest of needleleaf evergreen and broadleaf deciduous trees
- Broadleaf deciduous woodland
- Mid-latitude grassland
- Evergreen broadleaf and deciduous trees, shrubs and herbs
- Semi-desert scrub
- Desert
- Tropical grassland (savanna)
- Tropical broadleaf rainforest and needleleaf forest
- Sub-tropical broadleaf and needleleaf forest

NATURAL DISASTERS

- Locust invasion areas
- ■ Major famines
- ■ Major storms and floods

ENVIRONMENTAL CONCERNS

- Heavily polluted seas and lakes
- Other polluted seas and lakes
- Areas where the forest is being rapidly cut down (deforestation)
- Areas of continuous drought (deserts)
- Areas which are turning into desert due to soil erosion plus low rainfall (desertification)

Sahel '73
Sahel '73
Biafra '67
Ghana '83
Sudan '83
Ethiopia '73, '83
Bangladesh '73
Cambodia '84
Angola '84
Mozambique '87

Projection: *Hammer Equal Area*

THE GREENHOUSE EFFECT

Carbon dioxide is increased by burning fossil fuels and cutting forests

Carbon Dioxide

Rising temperatures would melt snow and ice.

Melting glacial ice could cause oceans to rise.

The carbon dioxide traps the heat being reflected from the Earth, although some heat is lost.

The warming increases water vapour in the air, leading to even greater absorption of heat.

VOLCANOES

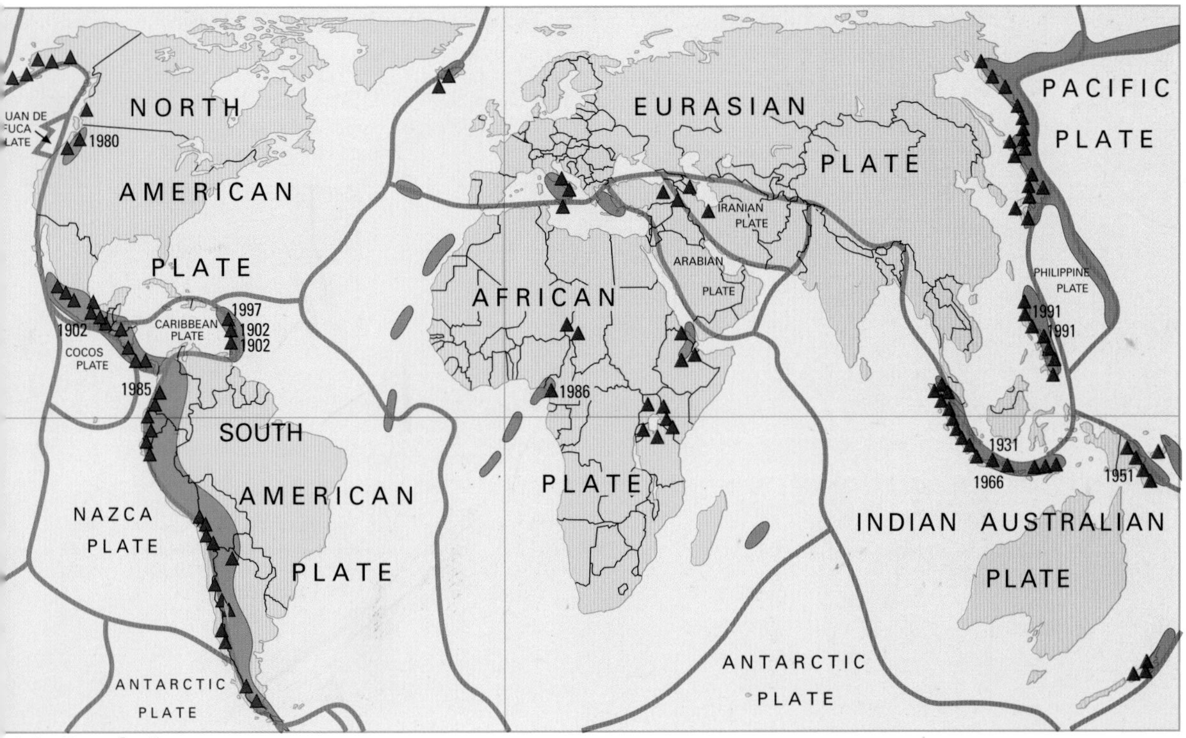

Volcanic regions

▲ Volcanoes (active since 1700)

Plate boundaries

ojection: *Hammer Equal Area*

OTORIOUS VOLCANIC ERUPTIONS

ear	Volcano	Deaths
79	Vesuvius, Italy	16,000
69	Mount Etna, Italy	20,000
72	Papandajan, Java	3,000
83	Skaptar Jökull, Iceland	10,000
1792	Unzen-Dake, Japan	15,000
1793	Miyi-Yama, Indonesia	50,000
1815	Tambora, Java	12,000
1883	Krakatoa, Indonesia	50,000
1902	Mount Pelée, Martinique	40,000
1902	Santa Maria, Guatemala	6,000
1902	Mount Taal, Philippines	1,400
1931	Merapi, Java	1,000
1951	Mount Lamington, Papua New Guinea	6,000
1966	Mount Kelud, Java	1,000
1980	Mount St. Helens, USA	100
1985	Nevado del Ruiz, Colombia	22,940
1986	Wum, Cameroon	1,700
1991	Mount Pinatubo, Philippines	300
1993	Mount Mayon, Philippines	77
1997	Soufrière Hills, Montserrat	23

EARTHQUAKES

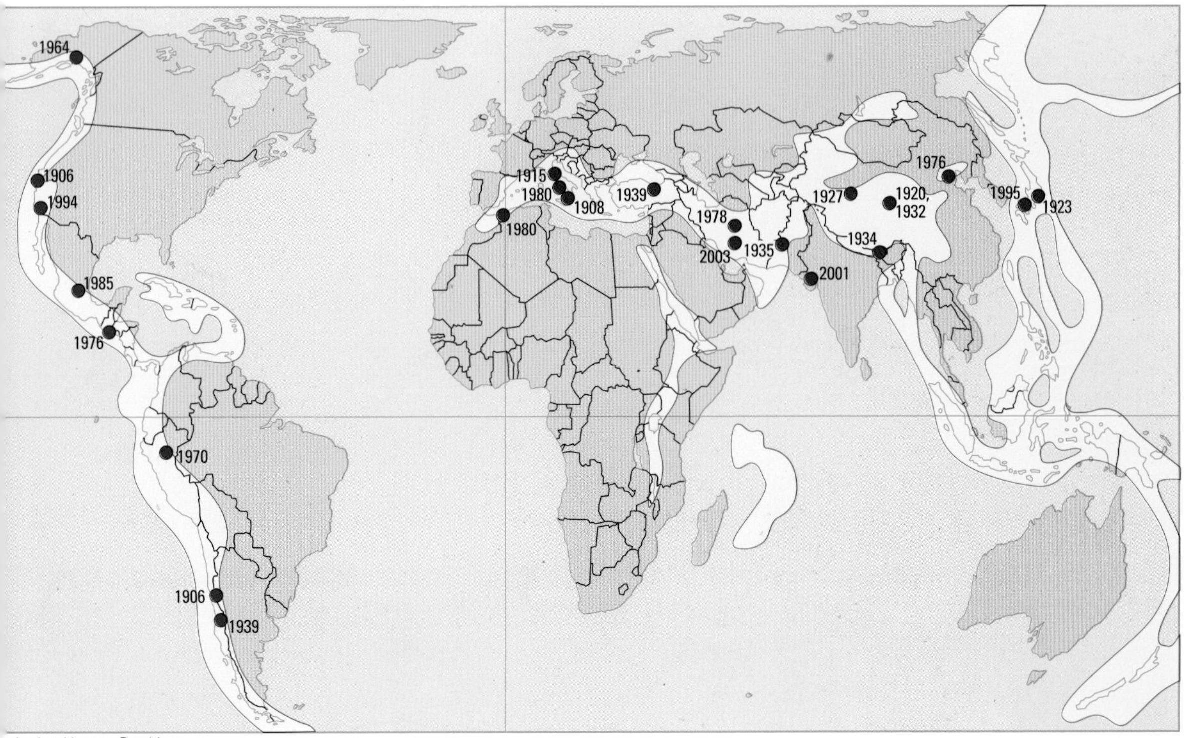

Earthquake regions

● Earthquakes (with dates)

ojection: *Hammer Equal Area*

OTORIOUS EARTHQUAKES SINCE 1900

ear	Location	Magnitude	Deaths
06	San Francisco, USA	8.3	503
06	Valparaiso, Chile	8.6	22,000
08	Messina, Italy	7.5	83,000
15	Avezzano, Italy	7.5	30,000
20	Gansu (Kansu), China	8.6	180,000
23	Yokohama, Japan	8.3	143,000
27	Nan Shan, China	8.3	200,000
32	Gansu (Kansu), China	7.6	70,000
34	Bihar, India/Nepal	8.4	10,700
1939	Quetta, India	7.5	60,000
1939	Chillan, Chile	8.3	28,000
1939	Erzincan, Turkey	7.9	30,000
1960	Agadir, Morocco	5.8	12,000
1964	Anchorage, Alaska	8.4	131
1970	Northern Peru	7.7	66,794
1972	Managua, Nicaragua	6.2	5,000
1974	Northern Pakistan	6.3	5,000
1976	Guatemala	7.5	22,778
1976	Tangshan, China	8.2	650,000
1978	Tabas, Iran	7.7	25,000
1980	El Asnam, Algeria	7.3	20,000
1980	Southern Italy	7.2	4,800
1985	Mexico City, Mexico	8.1	4,200
1988	Armenia	6.8	55,000
1990	Northern Iran	7.7	36,000
1993	Maharashtra, India	6.4	36,000
1994	Los Angeles, USA	6.6	57
1995	Kobe, Japan	7.2	5,000
1995	Sakhalin, Russia	7.5	2,000
1998	Rostaq, Afghanistan	7.0	5,000
1999	Izmit, Turkey	7.4	15,000
1999	Taipei, Taiwan	7.6	1,700
2001	Gujarat, India	7.7	16,800
2002	Baghlan, Afghanistan	6.1	1,000
2003	Bam, Iran	7.1	41,000

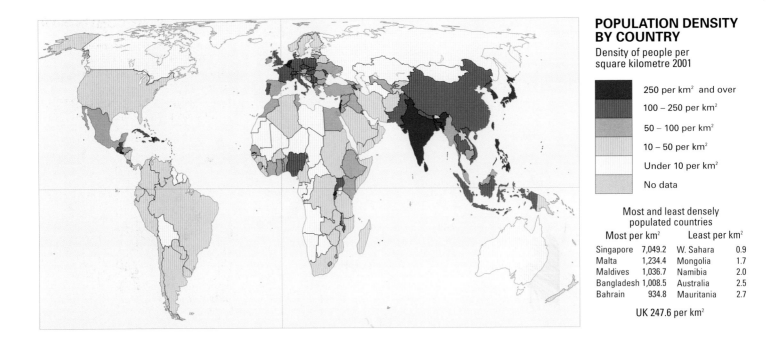

POPULATION DENSITY BY COUNTRY

Density of people per square kilometre 2001

	250 per km² and over
	100 – 250 per km²
	50 – 100 per km²
	10 – 50 per km²
	Under 10 per km²
	No data

Most and least densely populated countries

Most per km²		Least per km²	
Singapore	7,049.2	W. Sahara	0.9
Malta	1,234.4	Mongolia	1.7
Maldives	1,036.7	Namibia	2.0
Bangladesh	1,008.5	Australia	2.5
Bahrain	934.8	Mauritania	2.7

UK 247.6 per km²

POPULATION CHANGE

Change in total population 1990 – 2000

Over 40% gain	
20 – 40% gain	
10 – 20% gain	
0 – 10% gain	
Loss or no change	
No data	

Countries with the greatest population gains and losses (%)

Greatest gains		Greatest losses	
Kuwait	75.9	Germany	– 3.2
Namibia	69.4	Tonga	– 3.2
Afghanistan	60.1	Grenada	– 2.4
Mali	55.5	Hungary	– 0.2
Tanzania	54.6	Belgium	– 0.1

UK 2% gain

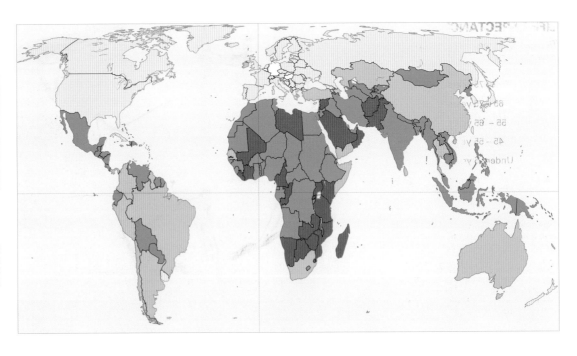

URBAN POPULATION

Percentage of total population living in towns and cities 2000

	80% urban and over
	60 – 80% urban
	40 – 60% urban
	20 – 40% urban
	Under 20% urban
	No data

Countries that are the most and least urbanized (%)

Most urbanized		Least urbanized	
Singapore	100	Rwanda	6.4
Nauru	100	Bhutan	7.3
Monaco	100	East Timor	7.4
Vatican City	100	Burundi	9.2
Belgium	97.3	Nepal	10.8

UK 89.3

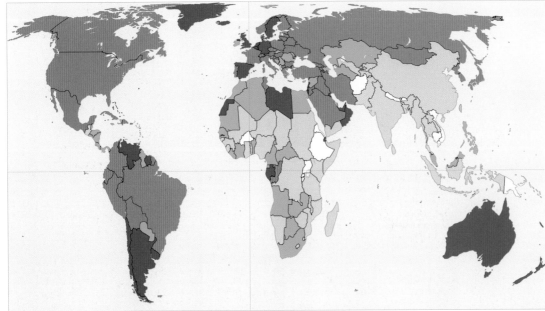
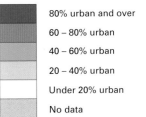

Projection: *Eckert IV*

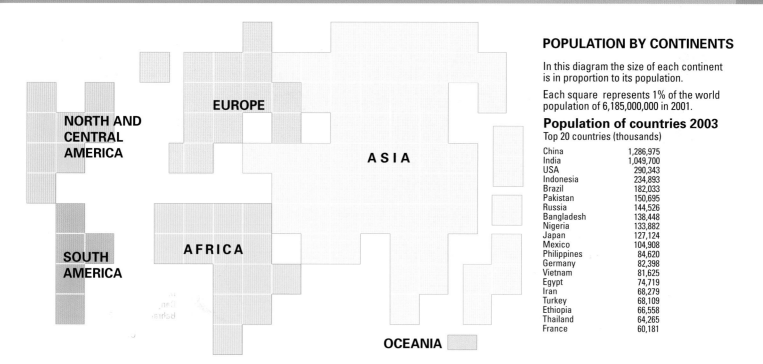

POPULATION BY CONTINENTS

In this diagram the size of each continent is in proportion to its population.

Each square represents 1% of the world population of 6,185,000,000 in 2001.

Population of countries 2003
Top 20 countries (thousands)

Country	Population
China	1,286,975
India	1,049,700
USA	290,343
Indonesia	234,893
Brazil	182,033
Pakistan	150,695
Russia	144,526
Bangladesh	138,448
Nigeria	133,882
Japan	127,124
Mexico	104,908
Philippines	84,620
Germany	82,398
Vietnam	81,625
Egypt	74,719
Iran	68,279
Turkey	68,109
Ethiopia	66,558
Thailand	64,265
France	60,181

LIFE EXPECTANCY

The average expected lifespan of babies born in 2001

- Over 75 years
- 65 – 75 years
- 55 – 65 years
- 45 – 55 years
- Under 45 years
- No data

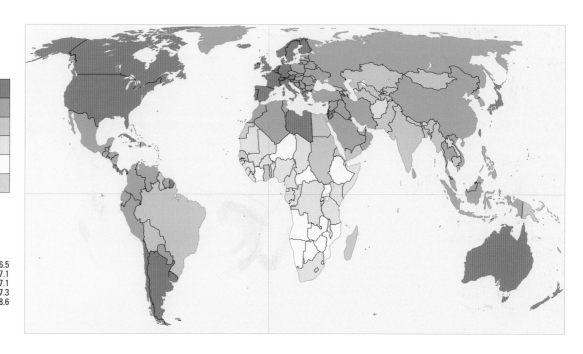

Highest life expectancy (years)		Lowest life expectancy (years)	
Andorra	83.5	Mozambique	36.5
San Marino	81.2	Botswana	37.1
Japan	80.8	Zimbabwe	37.1
Singapore	80.2	Zambia	37.3
Australia	79.9	Angola	38.6

UK 77.8 years

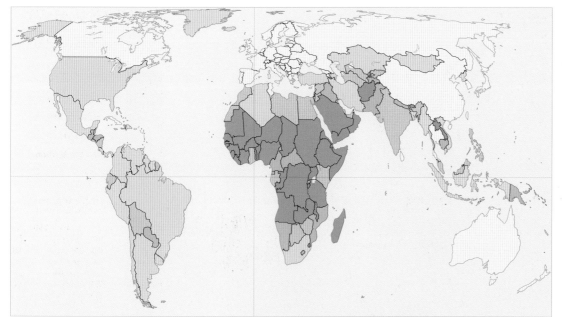

FAMILY SIZE

The average number of children a woman can expect to bear during her lifetime 2001

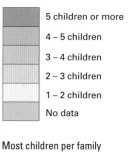

- 5 children or more
- 4 – 5 children
- 3 – 4 children
- 2 – 3 children
- 1 – 2 children
- No data

Most children per family

Somalia	7.1
Niger	7.1
Ethiopia	7.0
Yemen	7.0
Uganda	7.0

UK 1.7

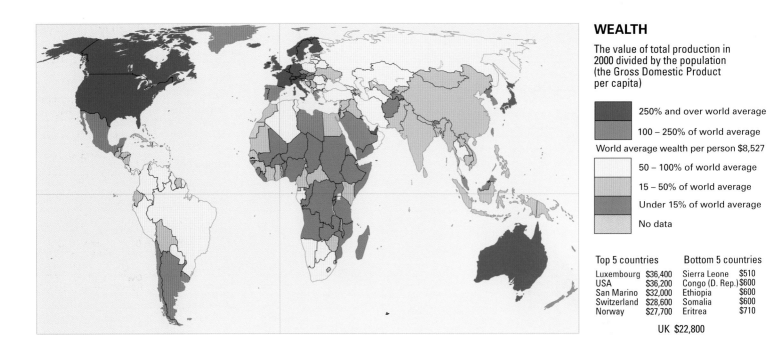

WEALTH

The value of total production in 2000 divided by the population (the Gross Domestic Product per capita)

- 250% and over world average
- 100 – 250% of world average

World average wealth per person $8,527

- 50 – 100% of world average
- 15 – 50% of world average
- Under 15% of world average
- No data

Top 5 countries		Bottom 5 countries	
Luxembourg	$36,400	Sierra Leone	$510
USA	$36,200	Congo (D. Rep.)	$600
San Marino	$32,000	Ethiopia	$600
Switzerland	$28,600	Somalia	$600
Norway	$27,700	Eritrea	$710

UK $22,800

WATER SUPPLY

The percentage of total population with access to safe drinking water 2000

- Over 90% with safe water
- 75 – 90% with safe water
- 60 – 75% with safe water
- 45 – 60% with safe water
- 30 – 45% with safe water
- Under 30% with safe water

Least well-provided countries

Afghanistan	13%
Ethiopia	24%
Chad	27%
Sierra Leone	28%
Cambodia	30%
Mauritania	37%

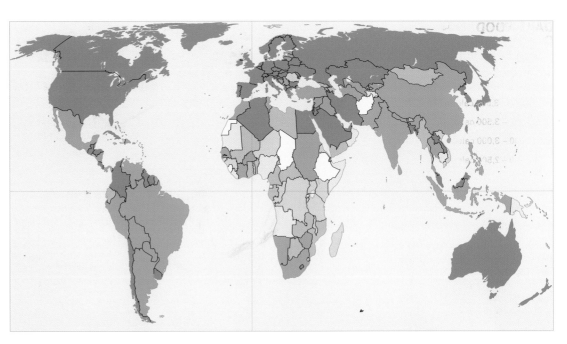

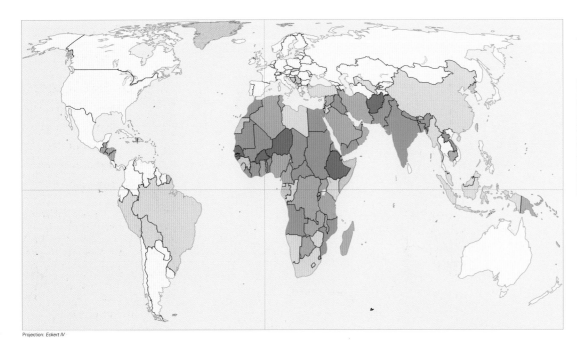

ILLITERACY

The percentage of total population unable to read or write 2000

- Over 60% are illiterate
- 40 – 60% are illiterate
- 20 – 40% are illiterate
- 10 – 20% are illiterate
- Under 10% are illiterate
- No data

Countries with the highest and lowest illiteracy rates

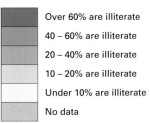

Highest (%)		Lowest (%)	
Niger	84	Australia	0
Burkina Faso	76	Denmark	0
Gambia	63	Estonia	0
Afghanistan	63	Finland	0
Senegal	63	Luxembourg	0

UK 1%

Projection: Eckert IV

EMPLOYMENT

Percentage of total Gross Domestic Product from service sector 1999

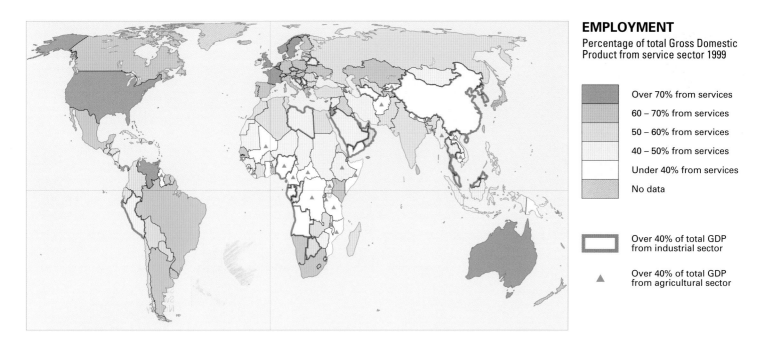

- Over 70% from services
- 60 – 70% from services
- 50 – 60% from services
- 40 – 50% from services
- Under 40% from services
- No data

- ▭ Over 40% of total GDP from industrial sector
- ▲ Over 40% of total GDP from agricultural sector

DAILY FOOD CONSUMPTION

Average daily food intake in calories per person 2000

- Over 3,500 calories
- 3,000 – 3,500 calories
- 2,500 – 3,000 calories
- 2,000 – 2,500 calories
- Under 2,000 calories
- No data

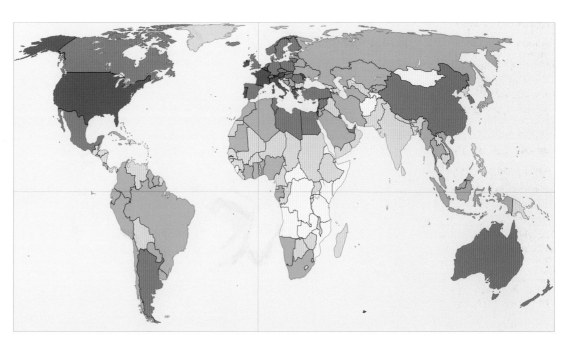

Top 5 countries		Bottom 5 countries	
Portugal	3,654	Somalia	1,573
Greece	3,617	Eritrea	1,627
Belgium	3,602	Burundi	1,687
Ireland	3,557	Afghanistan	1,732
Austria	3,555	Mozambique	1,682

U.K. 3,211

HEALTH CARE

Number of people per qualified doctor 1999

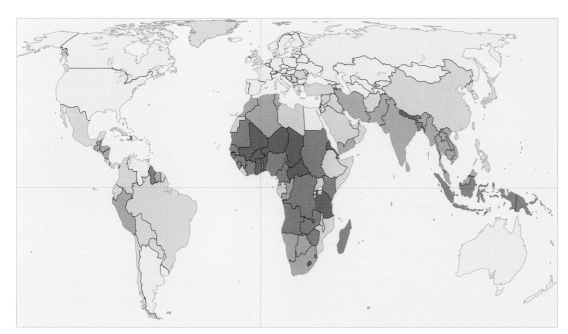

- Over 15,000 per doctor
- 5,000 – 15,000 per doctor
- 1,000 – 5,000 per doctor
- 500 – 1,000 per doctor
- Under 500 per doctor
- No data

Countries with the most and least people per doctor

Most people		Least people	
Eritrea	33,333	Italy	181
Chad	30,303	Belarus	226
Burkina Faso	29,412	Georgia	229
Niger	28,517	Spain	236
Tanzania	24,390	Russia	238

UK 610 people

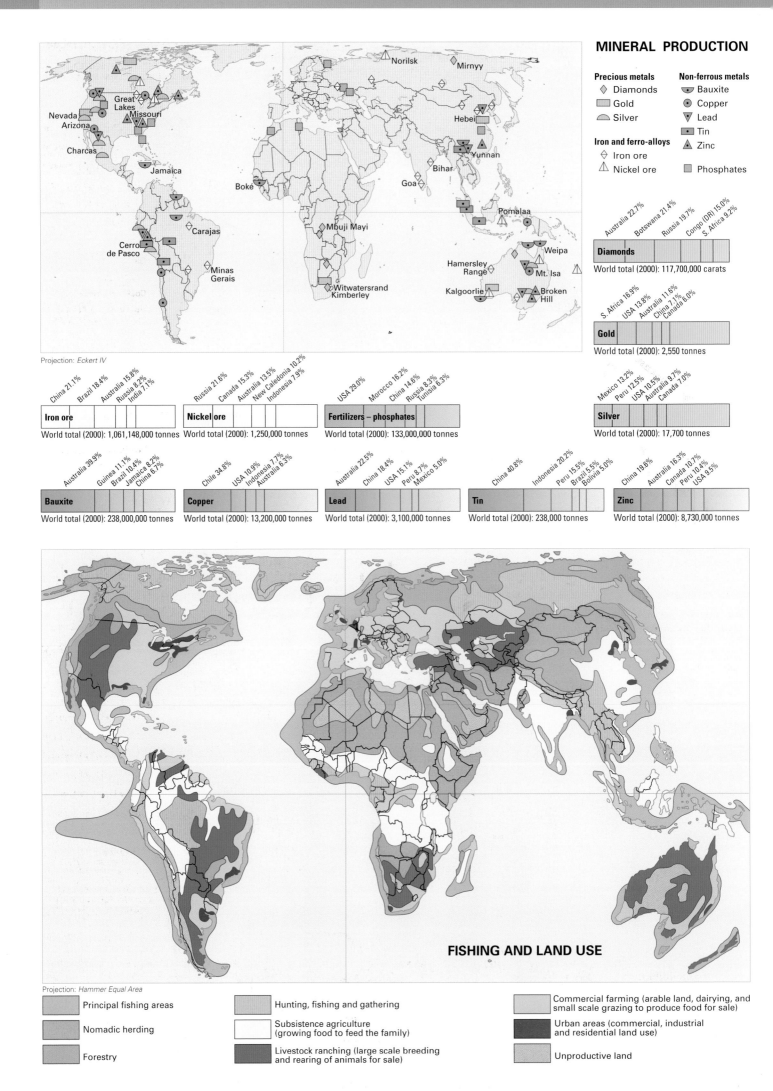

MINERAL PRODUCTION

Precious metals
◇ Diamonds
▭ Gold
◠ Silver

Iron and ferro-alloys
◇ Iron ore
△ Nickel ore

Non-ferrous metals
⬭ Bauxite
◉ Copper
▽ Lead
▪ Tin
▲ Zinc

▭ Phosphates

Diamonds
Australia 22.7% | Botswana 21.4% | Russia 19.7% | Congo (DR) 15.0% | S. Africa 9.2%
World total (2000): 117,700,000 carats

Gold
S. Africa 16.9% | USA 13.8% | Australia 11.6% | China 7.1% | Canada 6.0%
World total (2000): 2,550 tonnes

Silver
Mexico 13.2% | Peru 12.5% | USA 10.5% | Australia 9.7% | Canada 7.0%
World total (2000): 17,700 tonnes

Iron ore
China 21.1% | Brazil 18.4% | Australia 15.8% | Russia 8.2% | India 7.1%
World total (2000): 1,061,148,000 tonnes

Nickel ore
Russia 21.6% | Canada 15.3% | Australia 13.5% | New Caledonia 10.2% | Indonesia 7.9%
World total (2000): 1,250,000 tonnes

Fertilizers – phosphates
USA 29.0% | Morocco 16.2% | China 14.6% | Russia 8.3% | Tunisia 6.3%
World total (2000): 133,000,000 tonnes

Bauxite
Australia 39.9% | Guinea 11.1% | Brazil 10.4% | Jamaica 8.2% | China 6.7%
World total (2000): 238,000,000 tonnes

Copper
Chile 34.8% | USA 10.9% | Indonesia 7.7% | Australia 6.3%
World total (2000): 13,200,000 tonnes

Lead
Australia 22.5% | China 18.4% | USA 15.1% | Peru 8.7% | Mexico 5.0%
World total (2000): 3,100,000 tonnes

Tin
China 40.8% | Indonesia 20.2% | Peru 15.5% | Brazil 5.5% | Bolivia 5.0%
World total (2000): 238,000 tonnes

Zinc
China 19.6% | Australia 16.3% | Canada 10.7% | Peru 10.4% | USA 9.5%
World total (2000): 8,730,000 tonnes

Projection: *Eckert IV*

FISHING AND LAND USE

Projection: *Hammer Equal Area*

▭ Principal fishing areas

▭ Nomadic herding

▭ Forestry

▭ Hunting, fishing and gathering

▭ Subsistence agriculture (growing food to feed the family)

▭ Livestock ranching (large scale breeding and rearing of animals for sale)

▭ Commercial farming (arable land, dairying, and small scale grazing to produce food for sale)

▭ Urban areas (commercial, industrial and residential land use)

▭ Unproductive land

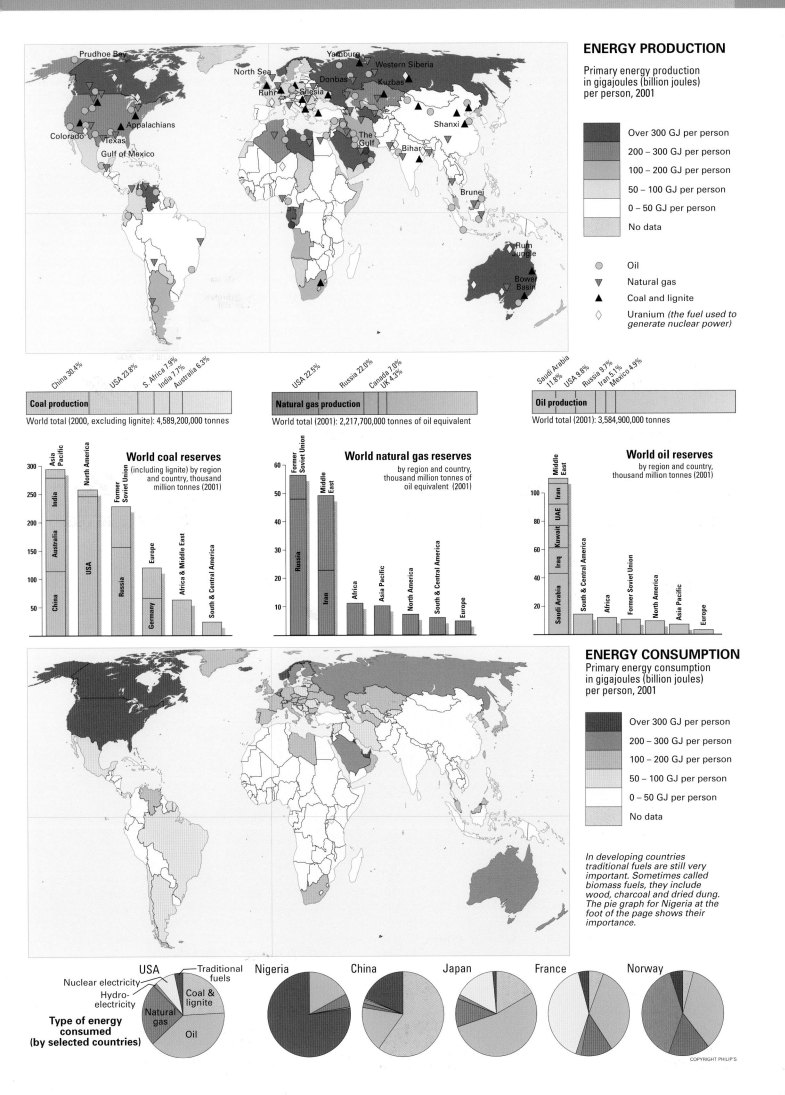

ENERGY PRODUCTION

Primary energy production
in gigajoules (billion joules)
per person, 2001

- Over 300 GJ per person
- 200 – 300 GJ per person
- 100 – 200 GJ per person
- 50 – 100 GJ per person
- 0 – 50 GJ per person
- No data

- ○ Oil
- ▽ Natural gas
- ▲ Coal and lignite
- ◇ Uranium *(the fuel used to generate nuclear power)*

Prudhoe Bay, North Sea, Yamburg, Western Siberia, Donbas, Ruhr, Silesia, Kuzbas, Shanxi, Appalachians, Colorado, Texas, Gulf of Mexico, The Gulf, Bihar, Brunei, Rum Jungle, Bower Basin

Coal production
China 30.4% | USA 23.8% | S. Africa 7.9% | India 7.7% | Australia 6.3%
World total (2000, excluding lignite): 4,589,200,000 tonnes

Natural gas production
USA 22.5% | Russia 22.0% | Canada 7.0% | UK 4.3%
World total (2001): 2,217,700,000 tonnes of oil equivalent

Oil production
Saudi Arabia 11.8% | USA 9.8% | Russia 9.7% | Iran 5.1% | Mexico 4.9%
World total (2001): 3,584,900,000 tonnes

World coal reserves
(including lignite) by region
and country, thousand
million tonnes (2001)

Asia Pacific (India, Australia, China), North America (USA), Former Soviet Union (Russia), Europe (Germany), Africa & Middle East, South & Central America

World natural gas reserves
by region and country,
thousand million tonnes of
oil equivalent (2001)

Former Soviet Union (Russia), Middle East (Iran), Africa, Asia Pacific, North America, South & Central America, Europe

World oil reserves
by region and country,
thousand million tonnes (2001)

Middle East (Saudi Arabia, Iraq, Kuwait, UAE, Iran), South & Central America, Africa, Former Soviet Union, North America, Asia Pacific, Europe

ENERGY CONSUMPTION

Primary energy consumption
in gigajoules (billion joules)
per person, 2001

- Over 300 GJ per person
- 200 – 300 GJ per person
- 100 – 200 GJ per person
- 50 – 100 GJ per person
- 0 – 50 GJ per person
- No data

*In developing countries
traditional fuels are still very
important. Sometimes called
biomass fuels, they include
wood, charcoal and dried dung.
The pie graph for Nigeria at the
foot of the page shows their
importance.*

USA — Nuclear electricity, Hydro-electricity, Traditional fuels, Coal & lignite, Natural gas, Oil

**Type of energy
consumed
(by selected countries)**

Nigeria   China   Japan   France   Norway

COPYRIGHT PHILIP'S

THE SEASONS

Seasons occur because the Earth's axis is tilted at an angle of approximately 23½°. In June, the northern hemisphere is tilted towards the Sun. As a result it receives more hours of sunshine in a day and therefore has its warmest season, summer. By December, the Earth has rotated halfway round the Sun so that the southern hemisphere is tilted towards the Sun and it has its summer. The hemisphere that is tilted away from the Sun has winter. On 21 June the Sun is directly overhead at the Tropic of Cancer, 23½°N, and this is midsummer in the northern hemisphere. Midsummer in the southern hemisphere occurs on 21 December, when the Sun is overhead at the Tropic of Capricorn.

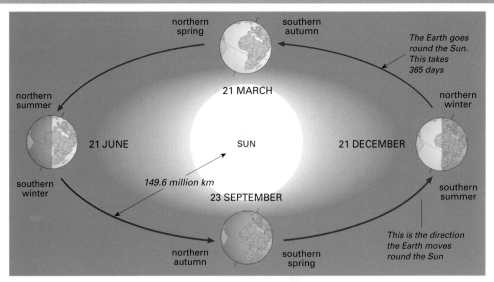

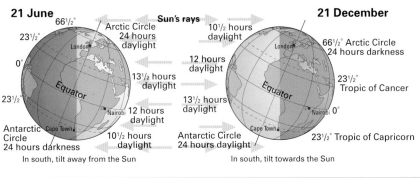

DAY AND NIGHT

The Sun appears to rise in the east, reach its highest point at noon, and then set in the west. In reality, it is not the Sun that is moving but the Earth rotating from west to east. Due to the tilting of the Earth, the length of day and night varies from place to place and month to month. In June the Arctic has constant daylight and the Antarctic has constant darkness. The situations are reversed in December. In the Tropics the length of day and night varies little throughout the year. The table below gives day and night lengths for three cities at different times of the year.

	March (Northern Spring Southern Autumn)			**June** (Northern Summer Southern Winter)			**September** (Northern Autumn Southern Spring)			**December** (Northern Winter Southern Summer)		
	London	Nairobi	Cape Town	London	Nairobi	Cape Town	London	Nairobi	Cape Town	London	Nairobi	Cape Town
City												
Latitude	51°N	1°S	34°S	51°N	1°S	34°S	51°N	1°S	34°S	51°N	1°S	34°S
Day length	12 hrs	12 hrs	12 hrs	16 hrs	12 hrs	10 hrs	12 hrs	12 hrs	12 hrs	8 hrs	12 hrs	14 hrs
Night length	12 hrs	12 hrs	12 hrs	8 hrs	12 hrs	14 hrs	12 hrs	12 hrs	12 hrs	16 hrs	12 hrs	10 hrs
Temperature	7°C	21°C	21°C	16°C	18°C	13°C	15°C	19°C	14°C	5°C	19°C	20°C

The Earth rotates through 360° in 24 hours, and so moves 15° every hour. The World is divided into 24 standard time zones, each centred on lines of longitude at 15° intervals. The Greenwich Meridian lies on the centre of the first zone. All places to the west of Greenwich are one hour behind for every 15° of longitude; places to the east are ahead by one hour for every 15°.

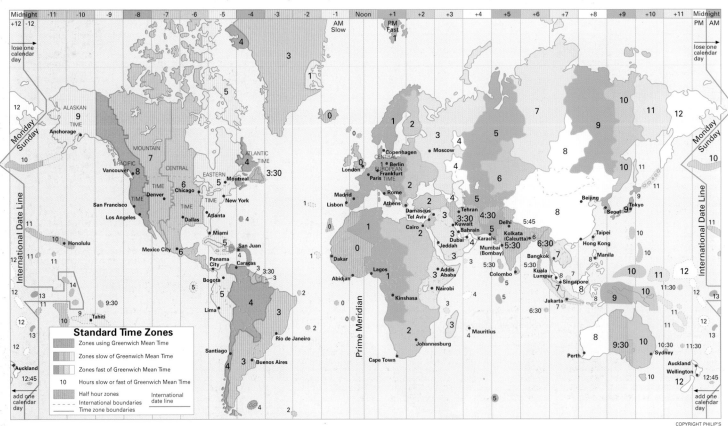

INDEX

This index is a list of all the names on the maps in the atlas. They are listed in alphabetical order. If a name has a description with it, for example, Bay of Biscay, the name is in alphabetical order, followed by the description:

> Biscay, Bay of ....

Sometimes, the same name occurs in more than one country. In these cases, the country names are added after each place name, and they are indexed alphabetically by country.
For example:

> Cordoba, Argentina .....
> Cordoba, Spain ....

All rivers are indexed to their mouths or confluences and are followed by the symbol ➤.

Each name in the index is followed by a number in **bold** type which refers to the number of the page the map appears on.

The figure and letter which follow the page number give the grid rectangle on the map within which the feature appears. The grid is formed by the lines of latitude and longitude. The columns are labelled at the top and bottom with a letter and the rows at the sides with a number. Wrocław for example, is in the grid square where row 5 crosses column D.

For more precise location on small scale maps the latitude and longitude are given after the figure/letter reference. The first set of figures represent the latitude, the second set of figures represent the longitude.

The unit of measurement for latitude and longitude is the degree (°), which is subdivided into minutes ('). Here only full degree figures are given. The latitude is followed by N(orth) or S(outh) of the Equator and the longitude by East or West of the prime meridian.
For example:

> Wrocław.........**35 5 D** 51°N 17°E

Aalborg	**36** 4 P 57N 9 E
Aarhus	**36** 4 P 56N 10 E
Abadan	**44** 3 C 30N 48 E
Abaetetuba	**30** 3 F 1S 48W
Abakan	**41** 10 D 53N 91 E
Abeokuta	**47** 10 L 7N 3 E
Aberdare	**5** 5 C 51N 3W
Aberdare Range	**26** 3 B 0S 36 E
Aberdeen	**6** 2 F 57N 2W
Aberystwyth	**5** 4 B 52N 4W
Abidjan	**46** 4 C 5N 3W
Abu Dhabi	**44** 4 D 24N 54 E
Abuja	**47** 10 M 9N 7 E
Acapulco	**54** 4 D 16N 99W
Accra	**47** 10 K 5N 0W
Accrington	**4** 3 D 53N 2W
Aconcagua	**51** 7 E 32S 70W
Acre	**30** 4 A 9S 71W
Adamawa Highlands	**47** 10 N 7N 12 E
Adana	**39** 4 L 37N 35 E
Addis Ababa	**46** 4 G 9N 38 E
Adelaide	**48** 6 F 34S 138 E
Aden	**44** 5 C 12N 45 E
Aden, Gulf of	**44** 5 C 12N 47 E
Adriatic Sea	**22** 3 F 43N 16 E
Aegean Sea	**39** 4 J 38N 25 E
Afghanistan	**44** 3 E 33N 65 E
Africa	**46** 5 F 10N 20 E
Agades	**46** 3 D 16N 7 E
Agra	**44** 4 F 27N 77 E
Aguanaval ➤	**54** 3 D 25N 102W
Aguascalientes	**54** 3 D 21N 102W
Agulhas, Cape	**28** 3 C 34S 20 E
Ahmadabad	**44** 4 F 23N 72 E
Ai-Ais and Fish River Canyon	**28** 2 B 27S 17 E
Aïr	**46** 3 D 18N 8 E
Airdrie	**6** 4 E 55N 3W
Aire ➤	**14** 5 F 53N 0W
Aix-en-Provence	**37** 11 L 43N 5 E
Ajaccio	**37** 12 M 41N 8 E
Akita	**43** 3 D 39N 140 E
Al Aziziyah	**46** 1 E 32N 13 E
Al Hufuf	**44** 4 C 25N 49 E
Al Jawf	**46** 2 F 24N 23 E
Alabama	**53** 4 J 33N 87W
Alabama ➤	**53** 4 J 31N 87W
Alagoas	**30** 4 H 9S 36W
Åland Islands	**35** 3 D 60N 20 E
Alaska	**50** 3 D 65N 150W
Alaska Peninsula	**50** 4 C 56N 160W
Alaska Range	**50** 3 D 62N 151W
Alaska, Gulf of	**50** 4 E 58N 145W
Albacete	**37** 13 H 39N 1W
Albania	**39** 3 G 41N 20 E
Albany	**48** 6 B 35S 117 E

Albert Nile ➤	**26** 2 A 3N 32 E
Albuquerque	**52** 3 E 35N 106W
Aldabra Islands	**46** 5 H 9S 46 E
Aldeburgh	**5** 4 H 52N 1 E
Alderney	**5** 7 D 49N 2W
Ålesund	**35** 3 B 62N 6 E
Aleutian Islands	**49** 2 K 52N 175W
Aleutian Trench	**49** 2 K 48N 180 E
Alexandria	**46** 1 G 31N 30 E
Algarve	**37** 14 G 36N 8W
Algeria	**46** 2 D 28N 2 E
Algiers	**46** 1 D 36N 3 E
Alicante	**37** 13 H 38N 0W
Alice Springs	**48** 4 E 23S 133 E
Allahabad	**44** 4 G 25N 81 E
Allegheny Mountains	**53** 3 L 38N 80W
Allen, Bog of	**7** 3 D 53N 7W
Allen, Lough	**7** 2 C 54N 8W
Alma Ata	**40** 8 E 43N 76 E
Almeria	**37** 14 G 36N 2W
Alnwick	**4** 1 E 55N 1W
Alps	**37** 9 N 46N 9 E
Altai	**40** 9 D 46N 92 E
Altamira	**30** 3 E 3S 52W
Amagasaki	**24** 2 D 34N 135 E
Amapá	**30** 2 E 2N 50W
Amazon ➤	**30** 3 E 0S 50W
Amazonas	**30** 4 B 5S 65W
America, North	**50** 5 K 45N 100W
America, South	**51** 5 F 10S 60W
Amiens	**37** 8 J 49N 2 E
Amlwch	**4** 3 B 53N 4W
Amritsar	**44** 3 F 31N 74 E
Amsterdam	**36** 6 L 52N 4 E
Amu Darya ➤	**40** 6 E 43N 59 E
Amur ➤	**41** 15 D 52N 141 E
An Uaimh	**7** 3 E 53N 6W
Anadyr Range	**41** 18 C 68N 175 E
Anápolis	**30** 6 F 16S 48W
Anchorage	**50** 3 E 61N 149W
Ancona	**22** 3 D 43N 13 E
Andaman Islands	**44** 5 H 12N 92 E
Andes	**51** 5 D 10S 75W
Andizhan	**40** 8 E 41N 72 E
Andorra	**37** 11 J 42N 1 E
Andover	**5** 5 E 51N 1W
Aneto, Pico de	**37** 11 J 42N 0 E
Angara ➤	**41** 10 D 58N 94 E
Angel Falls	**51** 3 E 5N 62W
Angers	**37** 9 H 47N 0W
Anglesey	**4** 3 B 53N 4W
Angola	**46** 6 E 12S 18 E
Angoulême	**37** 10 J 45N 0 E
Angus	**9** 3 E 56N 2W
Ankara	**39** 4 K 39N 32 E
Annaba	**38** 4 E 36N 7 E
Annan	**6** 5 E 54N 3W

Annan ➤	**6** 4 E 54N 3W
Annapolis	**53** 3 L 38N 76W
Anshan	**45** 2 L 41N 122 E
Antalya	**39** 4 K 36N 30 E
Antananarivo	**47** 6 H 18S 47 E
Antarctic Peninsula	**56** 2 L 67S 60W
Antarctica	**56** 2 D 90S 0W
Antigua	**55** 4 M 17N 61W
Antofagasta	**51** 6 D 23S 70W
Antrim	**7** 2 E 54N 6W
Antrim, Mountains of	**7** 2 E 54N 6W
Antwerp	**36** 7 L 51N 4 E
Aomori	**43** 2 D 40N 140 E
Apennines	**22** 3 D 44N 10 E
Appalachian Mountains	**53** 3 K 38N 80W
Appleby	**4** 2 D 54N 2W
Arabian Sea	**44** 5 E 16N 65 E
Aracaju	**30** 5 H 10S 37W
Araçatuba	**30** 7 E 21S 50W
Arafura Sea	**48** 2 E 9S 135 E
Araguaia ➤	**30** 4 F 5S 48W
Aral Sea	**40** 6 E 44N 60 E
Aran Island	**7** 2 C 55N 8W
Ararat, Mount	**34** 8 Q 39N 44 E
Arbroath	**6** 3 F 56N 2W
Arctic Ocean	**56** 1 B 78N 160W
Ardnamurchan, Point of	**6** 3 B 56N 6W
Ardrossan	**6** 4 D 55N 4W
Ards Peninsula	**7** 2 F 54N 5W
Arequipa	**51** 5 D 16S 71W
Argentina	**51** 7 E 35S 66W
Argyll & Bute	**9** 3 D 56N 5W
Arica	**51** 5 D 18S 70W
Aripuanã ➤	**30** 4 C 5S 60W
Arizona	**52** 4 D 34N 112W
Arkaig, Loch	**6** 3 C 56N 5W
Arkansas	**53** 4 H 35N 92W
Arkansas ➤	**53** 4 H 33N 91W
Arkhangelsk	**35** 3 J 64N 41 E
Arklow	**7** 4 E 52N 6W
Armagh	**7** 2 E 54N 6W
Armenia	**40** 5 E 40N 45 E
Arnhem	**36** 7 L 51N 5 E
Arnhem Land	**48** 2 E 13S 134 E
Arran	**6** 4 C 55N 5W
Aru Islands	**45** 7 M 6S 134 E
Arusha	**26** 3 B 3S 36 E
Asamankese	**47** 10 K 5N 0W
Ascension Island	**60** 5 J 8S 14W
Ashford	**5** 5 G 51N 0 E
Ashikaga	**24** 1 F 36N 139 E
Ashington	**4** 1 E 55N 1W
Ashizuri, Cape	**24** 3 C 32N 133 E
Ashkhabad	**40** 6 F 38N 57 E
Ashton under Lyne	**4** 3 D 53N 2W
Asmara	**46** 3 G 15N 38 E
Assam	**44** 4 H 26N 93 E

Astana	**40** 8 D 51N 71 E
Astrakhan	**40** 5 D 46N 48 E
Asunción	**51** 6 F 25S 57W
Aswan	**46** 2 G 24N 32 E
Asyût	**46** 2 G 27N 31 E
Atacama Desert	**51** 6 D 24S 69W
Athens	**39** 4 H 37N 23 E
Athlone	**7** 3 D 53N 7W
Athy	**7** 4 E 53N 7W
Atlanta	**53** 4 K 33N 84W
Atlantic Ocean	**60** 3 G 0 20W
Atlas Mountains	**46** 1 C 32N 5W
Auasberg	**28** 1 B 22S 17 E
Auckland	**48** 10 M 36S 174 E
Augsburg	**37** 8 P 48N 10 E
Augusta	**53** 2 N 44N 69W
Auob ➤	**28** 2 B 25S 19 E
Austin	**52** 4 G 30N 97W
Australia	**48** 4 E 23S 135 E
Austria	**38** 2 F 47N 14 E
Aviemore	**6** 2 E 57N 3W
Avignon	**37** 11 L 43N 4 E
Avon ➤, Bristol	**5** 5 D 51N 2W
Avon ➤, Hampshire	**5** 6 E 50N 1W
Avon ➤, Warwickshire	**14** 5 F 51N 2W
Awe, Loch	**6** 3 C 56N 5W
Ayers Rock	**48** 5 E 25S 131 E
Aylesbury	**5** 5 F 51N 0W
Ayr	**6** 4 D 55N 4W
Azerbaijan	**40** 5 E 40N 48 E
Azores	**60** 3 H 38N 29W
Azov, Sea of	**39** 2 L 46N 36 E
Bacabal	**30** 3 G 4S 44W
Bacău	**39** 2 J 46N 26 E
Badajoz	**37** 13 E 38N 6W
Baffin Bay	**50** 2 N 72N 64W
Baffin Island	**50** 2 M 68N 75W
Bagé	**30** 9 E 31S 54W
Baghdad	**44** 3 C 33N 44 E
Bahamas	**55** 3 J 24N 75W
Bahia	**30** 5 G 12S 42W
Bahía Blanca	**51** 7 E 38S 62W
Bahrain	**44** 4 D 26N 50 E
Baikal, Lake	**41** 11 D 53N 108 E
Baja California	**52** 4 C 31N 115W
Baku	**40** 6 E 40N 49 E
Balearic Islands	**37** 13 J 39N 3 E
Bali	**45** 7 K 8S 115 E
Balikeşir	**39** 4 J 39N 27 E
Balkan Mountains	**39** 3 H 43N 23 E
Balkhash, Lake	**40** 8 E 46N 74 E
Ballachulish	**6** 3 C 56N 5W
Ballarat	**48** 7 G 37S 143 E
Ballater	**6** 2 E 57N 3W
Ballina	**7** 2 B 54N 9W